Assessing Skills and Practice

D1555544

Students in higher education today are expected to demonstrate a wide range of skills and abilities to show that they have mastered not only subject content but also the ability to put their learning into practice in real-life contexts. This book explores how university staff can assess skills and practice skills fairly, effectively, efficiently and imaginatively.

Drawing on the expertise and experience of the authors and contributors through a wide range of international case studies, *Assessing Skills and Practice* provides theoretical perspectives on skills assessment. Topics discussed include:

- inclusive assessment – ensuring that all students achieve their maximum potential
- assessing across the arts, humanities and sciences – from lab work to dance
- the importance of involving all stakeholders (peers, employers, clients and tutors) in assessment
- how formative feedback helps students understand what is required of them

With pragmatic advice on implementation, *Assessing Skills and Practice* is ideal as an introduction for new or part-time lecturers, and students of PGCHE programmes. It will also be valued by experienced teachers new to this area of assessment or looking to improve their current practice, as well as course leaders, managers and those working on assessment related projects.

Ruth Pickford is a UK National Teaching Fellow and has twelve years' experience as a lecturer in information systems in both HE and FE. She is currently working with Innovation North and the CETL Institute for Enterprise at Leeds Metropolitan University developing initiatives to improve innovation and creativity in the student population.

Sally Brown is Pro Vice Chancellor at Leeds Metropolitan University with responsibility for assessment, learning and teaching and is visiting Professor at the Robert Gordon University.

Key Guides for Effective Teaching in Higher Education Series

Edited by Kate Exley

This indispensable series is aimed at new lecturers, postgraduate students who have teaching time, graduate teaching assistants, part-time tutors and demonstrators, as well as experienced teaching staff who may feel it's time to review their skills in teaching and learning.

Titles in this series will provide the teacher in higher education with practical, realistic guidance on the various different aspects of their teaching role, which is underpinned not only by current research in the field, but also by the extensive experience of individual authors, with a keen eye kept on the limitations and opportunities therein. By bridging a gap between academic theory and practice, all titles will provide generic guidance on teaching, learning and assessment issues which is then brought to life through the use of short illustrative examples drawn from a range of disciplines. All titles in this series will:

- represent up-to-date thinking and incorporate the use of communication and information technologies (C&IT) where appropriate;
- consider methods and approaches for teaching and learning when there is an increasing diversity in learning and a growth in student numbers;
- encourage reflective practice and self-evaluation, and a means of developing the skills of teaching, learning and assessment;
- provide links and references to further work on the topic and research evidence where appropriate.

Titles in the series will prove invaluable whether they are used for self-study or as part of a formal induction programme on teaching in higher education, and will also be of relevance to teaching staff working in further education settings.

Other titles in this series:

Assessing Students' Written Work: Marking Essays and Reports
– Catherine Haines
Designing Learning: From Module Outline to Effective Teaching
– Chris Butcher, Clara Davies and Melissa Highton
Developing Your Teaching: Ideas, Insight and Action
– Peter Kahn and Lorraine Walsh
Giving a Lecture: From Presenting to Teaching
– Kate Exley and Reg Dennick
Small Group Teaching
– Kate Exley and Reg Dennick
Using C&IT to Support Teaching
– Paul Chin

Assessing Skills and Practice

Ruth Pickford and
Sally Brown

Routledge
Taylor & Francis Group

LONDON AND NEW YORK

First published 2006
by Routledge
2 Park Square, Milton Park, Abingdon, Oxon OX14 4RN

Simultaneously published in the USA and Canada
by Routledge
270 Madison Ave, New York, NY 10016

Routledge is an imprint of the Taylor & Francis Group, an informa business

© 2006 Ruth Pickford and Sally Brown

Typeset in Perpetua and Bell Gothic by
Florence Production Ltd, Stoodleigh, Devon
Printed and bound in Great Britain by
TJ International Ltd, Padstow, Cornwall

British Library Cataloguing in Publication Data
A catalogue record for this book is available from the British Library

Library of Congress Cataloging in Publication Data
A catalog record for this book has been requested

ISBN10: 0–415–39400–7 (hbk)
ISBN10: 0–415–39399–X (pbk)
ISBN10: 0–203–96980–4 (ebk)

ISBN13: 978–0–415–39400–0 (hbk)
ISBN13: 978–0–415–39399–7 (pbk)
ISBN13: 978–0–203–96980–9 (ebk)

This book is dedicated to Elizabeth, Christopher and Sarah Pickford; to their dad Jonathan; and to their Grandma and Grandad for making life sweet.

Contents

Figures

Series preface

This series of books grew out of discussions with new lecturers and part-time teachers in universities and colleges who were keen to develop their teaching skills. However, experienced colleagues may also enjoy and find merit in the books, particularly the discussions about current issues that are impacting on teaching and learning in FE and HE, e.g. Widening Participation, disability legislation and the integration of C&IT in teaching.

New lecturers are now likely to be required by their institutions to take part in teaching development programmes. This frequently involves attending workshops, investigating teaching through mini-projects and reflecting on their practice. Many teaching programmes ask participants to develop their own teaching portfolios and to provide evidence of their developing skills and understanding. Scholarship of teaching is usually an important aspect of the teaching portfolio. New teachers can be asked to consider their own approach to teaching in relation to the wider literature, research findings and theory of teaching and learning. However, when people are beginning their teaching careers a much more pressing need may be to design and deliver an effective teaching session for tomorrow. Hence the intention of this series is to provide a complementary mix of very practical teaching tips and guidance together with a strong basis and clear rationale for their use.

In many institutions the numbers of part-time and occasional teachers actually outnumber the full-time staff. Yet the provision of formal training and development for part-time teachers is more sporadic and variable across the sector. As a result, this diverse group of educators can feel isolated and left out of the updating and support offered to their full-time counterparts. Never have there been so many part-time teachers involved in the design and delivery of courses, the support and guidance of students and the monitoring and assessment of learning. The group includes the thousands of post-graduate students who work as lab-demonstrators, problem class tutors, project supervisors and class teachers. It also includes clinicians, lawyers and professionals who contribute their specialist knowledge and skills to enrich the learning experience for many vocational and professional course students. Also included are the many hourly paid and jobbing tutors who have helped full-time staff cope with the expansion and diversification of HE and FE.

Universities sometimes struggle to know how many part-time staff they employ to teach and, as a group, occasional teachers are notoriously difficult to systematically contact through university and college communication systems. Part-time and occasional teachers often have other roles and responsibilities and teaching is a small but important part of what they do each day. Many part-time tutors would not expect to undertake the full range of teaching activities of full-time staff but may well do lots of tutoring or lots of class teaching but never lecture or supervise (or vice versa). So the series provides short practical books focusing very squarely on different teaching roles and activities. The first four books published are:

- Assessing Students' Written Work: Marking Essays and Reports
- Giving a Lecture: From Presenting to Teaching
- Small Group Teaching
- Using C&IT to Support Teaching

The books are all very practical with detailed discussion of teaching techniques and methods but they are based upon educational theory and research findings. Articles are referenced, further readings and related web sites are given and workers in the field are quoted and acknowledged. To this end Dr George Brown has been commissioned to produce an associated web-based guide on Student Learning which can be freely accessed by readers to accompany the books and provide a substantial foundation for the teaching and assessment practices discussed and recommended for the texts.

There is much enthusiasm and support here too for the excellent work currently being carried out by the Higher Education Academy subject centres within discipline groupings (indeed, individual subject centres are suggested as sources of further information throughout these volumes). The need to provide part-time tutors with realistic connections with their own disciplines is keenly felt by all the authors in the series and 'how it might work in your department' examples are given at the end of many of the activity-based chapters. However, there is no doubt some merit in sharing teaching developments across the boundaries of disciplines, culture and country as many of the problems in the tertiary education sector are themselves widely shared.

UNDERLYING THEMES

The use of Computing and Information Technology (C&IT) to enrich student learning and to help manage the workload of teachers is a recurring theme in the series. I acknowledge that not all teachers may yet have access to state-of-the-art teaching resources and facilities. However, the use of Virtual Learning Environments, e-learning provision and audio-visual presentation media is now widespread in universities.

The books also acknowledge and try to help new teachers respond to the growing and changing nature of the student population. Students with non-traditional backgrounds, international students, students who have disabilities or special needs are encouraged through the government's Widening Participation agenda to take part in Further and Higher Education. The books seek to advise teachers on current legislative requirements and offer guidance on recommended good practice on teaching diverse groups of students.

These were our goals and I and my co-authors sincerely hope these volumes prove to be a helpful resource for colleagues, both new and experienced, in HE.

Acknowledgements

This book would not have been produced without the co-ordination skills and cheerful support of Deb Chapman. Thanks too to Kate Exley, the Series Editor, Heather Clothier and Phil Race who also contributed significantly.

Our thanks also go to:

Kristine Mason O'Connor, University of Gloucester
Melanie Parker, Judith Waterfield and SPACE, University of Plymouth
Val Farrar, Newcastle University
Roger Willison and Lara Morgan, Nottingham University
John Rearden, Alison Price, Pete Rodgers, Dave Rodgers, Simon Sharpe, Janice Forder, Ollie Jones, Ted Sarmiento, Linda Shaw, Lesley Earle, John Gray, Dianne Willis and members of Innovation North Faculty at Leeds Metropolitan University
Mike Adams, Disability Rights Commission
Frank Lyons, Portsmouth University
Kay Sambell and Anntain Hubbard, Northumbria University
Marion Bowl
Lowri Blake, Royal College of Music
Ian Hughes, Leeds University
Andrew Ireland, Bournemouth Media School
Geoffrey Baxter, University of Ulster
David Walter, Liverpool Hope University
Paul Bartholomew, University of Central England
Bernard Moss, Staffordshire University
Nigel Duncan, City University London

Introduction
Assessing skills and practice:
key issues

Assessment of undergraduate (and to a lesser extent postgraduate) students is changing. Universities in the past were concerned principally with teaching and assessing high-level content, with a focus on skills only found in a relatively limited range of vocational and professional courses. Courses and programmes offered by higher education institutions (HEIs) today cover a broader range of subjects, many of them practically oriented, so live and practical skills are increasingly taught and measured at degree level. Additionally, it has become an expectation that HEIs should develop and assess a range of what are variously termed key, common or core skills. These include *inter alia* effective communication orally and in writing, problem solving, information retrieval and management, the ability to work independently and as a member of a team, leadership, entrepreneurship, time- and self-management and creativity. Experience at Alverno College, a small US college of higher education with an international reputation for fostering and assessing skills systemically, has hugely influenced international practice on the integration and progressive development of skills within the curriculum (Mentkowski 2000). These skills are sometimes taught explicitly, but more often are expected to be developed independently as part of maturing 'graduateness' and they increasingly form part of the assessment diet. This book is about the assessment of a wide range of live and practical skills, mainly focusing on skills associated with vocational and professional courses, but also including reference to the assessment of skills in practice that any student might be expected to demonstrate at higher education (HE) level.

Students nowadays are expected to demonstrate skills and abilities that show they have mastered not only subject content but also the ability to put their learning into practice in real-life contexts. Major initiatives in a number of countries, including the UK, focus on fostering students' employability, and research indicates that employers prefer to employ graduates who can demonstrate professionally related competencies as well as more general key skills. In a range of professional and practical disciplines the 'ability to do' is equally important as the 'ability to know'. These include not only traditional disciplines including law, medicine, surveying and performance arts but also newer disciplines including electronic games design and complementary medicine.

Traditionally, some HE practitioners have been much more comfortable assessing the knowledge content of programmes rather than the skills base they aim to foster concurrently. There has been a growing recognition of the necessity to assess capability as a central element of the HE experience. At the same time, higher education institutions have been working towards re-engineering the curriculum in order to integrate skills development and the recording of students' achievement in ways that are meaningful and useful. This book suggests ways in which new and experienced HE staff can assess live and practical skills in ways that are fair, reliable, valid, authentic, efficient and manageable. This is part of a move towards constructive alignment of the curriculum (Biggs 2003), which aims to ensure that what is taught is relevant and outcomes-orientated, as well as being usefully reflected within the assessment processes.

Some forms of assessment are more difficult than others to design and manage. Assessing short answers when provided with a set of correct responses, or working through mathematical problems using model answers is often tedious but rarely taxing. Other forms of assessment are much more demanding, particularly when evaluative skill is needed to make judgements about the quality of the work. The majority of assessment in higher education in many countries has, since the nineteenth century, been undertaken using unseen time-constrained examinations. This still remains the case in most countries, but increasingly HE practitioners are exploring other ways to measure and record achievement, especially when authentic assessment of practical skills is sought.

STRUCTURE OF THIS BOOK

This book is designed both to explore the issues underlying effective assessment of skills and practice and to offer pragmatic guidance on how best to undertake this, while also offering examples of good practice in the form of case studies, sample proformas and other documentation.

In the first section, we explore a range of issues concerned with effective assessment design. Chapter 1 asks how we can design assignments that align fully with relevant and appropriate learning outcomes and are also fit for purpose, assessing skills and practice authentically and validly. Formative assessment is essential for programmes that include skills and practice. High importance is frequently given to ensuring that students' activities and behaviours are shaped and improved by formative developmental advice and helpful critique prior to summative marking/grading. Chapter 2 considers how we can make assessment really integral to learning by using it formatively, since research indicates that this is likely to lead to improved retention and performance (Yorke and Longden 2004, Sadler 1998).

Good assessment design benefits all students. Assessment should be designed to be inclusive from the outset, rather than trying to deal with diversity by exception. Chapter 3 deals with ensuring equivalence of experience for disabled students, which is not simply a matter of social justice but is also in many countries a legal imperative. Chapter 4 discusses inclusive assessment in relation to other kinds of diversity including age, gender and ethnicity. We can never eliminate bias and subjectivity altogether, but we can develop our own awareness of likely sources of injustice and build in safeguards against it at the design stage.

The second section looks at a range of contexts in which assessment of skills and practice takes place. Students working in practical domains frequently have to structure their own working lives in the studio, lab or workplace, so Chapter 5 discusses how we can promote independent learning skills by incorporating these into assessed tasks. Such skills are not automatically linked to high achievement in pre-HE programmes, so fostering them is valuable in terms of both promoting self-confidence and working towards higher levels of student retention, particularly among students from disadvantaged backgrounds.

Most HE programmes include an element of assessment of oral and presentation skills and we explore how best to do this in Chapter 6, looking particularly at how to assess fairly and effectively, making best use of staff time.

In Chapter 7 we argue for practices in assessing practical skills in laboratories that are meaningful and productive in terms of learning. Traditionally many students find writing up 'labs' for assessment a gruelling and meaningless chore: here we propose some alternatives that can make assessment more relevant, and more efficient in terms of staff time.

In Chapter 8 the topic under consideration is the assessment of arte-facts in the studio and workshop. This is an area which, in the past, has relied heavily on individual judgement, often against internal rather than externally expressed criteria. Our suggestions here are designed to work towards higher levels of validity and consistency and to help students understand more fully how these judgements are achieved. Similar issues are covered in Chapter 9, where we consider the assessment of live performances. Helping students understand the rationale behind assess-ment decisions made about their work is highly likely to lead to improved performance and will also give them confidence that our judgements are fair and transparent, based soundly on criteria that they can recognise.

We look in the final section at agency, with a discussion of who is best placed to assess process in Chapter 10. We are convinced that students learn better and become more effective as lifelong learners if they become involved in their own and others' assessment, so we concentrate here on the pragmatics and potential benefits of using peer assessment of processes and outcomes. Chapter 11 follows, with a discussion of how we can use other stakeholders, including employers, placement tutors and clients to assess skills and practice consistently, recognising the com-plexity of working with multiple assessors off campus.

We conclude this volume in Chapter 12 with a brief manifesto which summarises the values underpinning the practice outlined in this book. This serves both as a rationale for our work and as an agenda for delib-eration that can be used for staff development workshops on the assessment of skills and practice. We hope that this, and the rest of the volume, will be of use to our readers, whether experienced prac-titioners looking for some new ideas or novices in the first stages of teaching careers seeking pragmatic guidance.

Chapter 1

The importance of good practical assessment design

> Assessment methods and requirements probably have a greater influence on how and what students learn than any other single factor. This influence may well be of greater importance than the impact of teaching materials.
>
> (Boud 1988)

As Boud argues: if you get the assessment right, you are likely to direct students' activities appropriately. Students gain cues about what you value from the assignments/tasks you set and will direct their out-of-class learning activities accordingly. If we focus the tasks we set them on recall and memorisation, that's what they'll do! If, however, we want to encourage them to take a deep rather than a surface approach to the development of practical skills, we need to design practical assignments intelligently. We need to think not just about the assessment criteria but also about weighting, timing, agency and 'fitness for purpose', with imaginative consideration of methods and approaches that can challenge students, be inclusive and suit the topic, context, cohort and level. Practical assessments should link clearly to the most sensible *evidence of practical skill* our students could produce to demonstrate their achievement of the intended outcome. Essential to all forms of assessment is clarity about criteria, and this is particularly the case when the assessor is considering the extent to which practical skills have been satisfactorily demonstrated.

DESIGNING FIT-FOR-PURPOSE PRACTICAL ASSESSMENTS

Authentic practical assessment which genuinely assesses what it sets out to assess needs to use 'fit-for-purpose' assessment approaches. When

1

designing any practical assessment instrument, process or strategy we should be seeking answers to a series of questions that can help to make the design of assignments systematic, coherent and aligned with our intentions (Box 1.1).

Box 1.1
FIT-FOR-PURPOSE PRACTICAL ASSESSMENT QUESTIONS

Why are we assessing?
- What are our particular purposes for understanding the task on this occasion?
- To give feedback?
- To help students to adjust their practice?
- To make a pass/fail decision?
- To motivate or reinforce practice?
- To grade or categorise students?
- To testify regarding fitness-to-practice?
- To enable informed option or career choice?
- To help students know how they are doing?
- To help them know where they need to direct their energies?
- To remediate errors and modify inappropriate behaviours?
- To review under-pinning values?
- To help us know what impact our teaching is having?

What is it we are assessing?
- Is the focus on product, outcome or process, or the use of theory in practice?
- How important is the means by which the practical outcome is achieved?
- Does it make sense to assess work in progress as well as the finished product?
- Is group work or teamwork an important component of the achievement?
- How important is originality/creativity?
- To what extent is conformance with standards important?

How are we assessing?
- What methods and approaches can we use?

- Should we be using vivas, presentations, portfolios, in-tray exercises, case-studies, posters, production of artefacts, performances, annotated bibliographies, surveys, projects, laboratory activities, live or simulated interaction with clients/patients?
- Is group, self or peer assessment appropriate?
- How useful would computer-assisted assessment be?
- Is online assessment a possibility?

Who is best placed to assess?

- Tutors usually undertake tasks requiring judgement, but are there opportunities for peers from other groups (i.e. *inter-peer group assessment*) or from within one's own group (i.e. *intra-peer group assessment*) to be involved?
- To what extent can self-assessment be incorporated?
- And, particularly with practical skills, how far can employers, clients and workplace line managers be involved?
- What about audiences at performances or visitors to exhibitions, displays and installations?

When should assessment take place?

- Must it be end point (once the student has more or less finished with the subject)?
- Can it be incremental, at intervals through the learning experience?
- Can students have several goes at the same practical assessment without penalty?
- To what extent is it important to align with the traditional academic year?
- Is it possible to accommodate accelerated progress through a programme?
- To what extent can accreditation of prior learning be incorporated?

If we want to assess capability, is it enough to assess it once, or do we need to be reassured that the competence is repeatable (other than just a lucky one-off success)? In professional areas like medicine or aeronautical engineering, most of us would agree that a single incident of success would not be reassuringly comprehensive!

3

INTERLOCKING QUESTIONS THAT UNDERPIN ASSESSMENT DESIGN

If we are to be convinced of capability, we need to have evidence of the achievement of the learning outcomes. Outcomes-based programmes are familiar to most people working in HEIs nowadays, and the satisfactory achievement of these outcomes is normally used as a proxy for competence. However, badly designed learning outcomes can be difficult to assess if they are:

- vague, woolly, over-ambiguous or bland;
- tangential to what it is really intended that students should achieve;
- multiple, so that the assessor is flummoxed by partial achievement;
- expressed in excessively complex polysyllabic Latinate terminology;
- inappropriate in terms of level, scope or extent.

Assessment is not just a final summative act at the end of a learning process. It should be integral to learning. Too often, how a programme is to be assessed is an afterthought at the end of a creative and detailed curriculum design process.

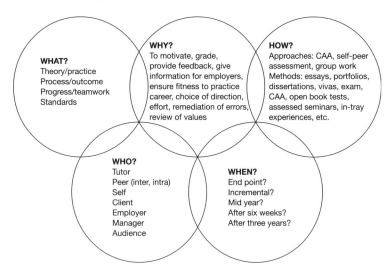

FIGURE 1.1 Interlocking questions that underpin assessment design

Additionally, hard-pressed course designers tend to fall back on tried (frequently) and tested (rarely) approaches which use conventional methods, because that's the kind of thing they've always done in the past.

To be genuinely effective, we need to turn the curriculum design process on its head, linking the anticipated evidence of achievement of the intended learning outcomes with assessment design from the outset, and moving on to detailed content and delivery planning once this has been achieved (Figure 1.1).

> Despite the good intentions of staff, assessment tasks are set which encourage a narrow instrumental approach to learning that emphasises the reproduction of what is presented at the expense of critical thinking, deep understanding and independent activity.
>
> (Boud 1990: 104)

Effective assessment of practical skills should be:

Valid: measuring as closely as possible the evidence of achievement of the intended learning outcomes in as fit-for-purpose a way as possible. In other words, are we measuring exactly what we intend to measure?

Reliable: ensuring that marking schemes and criteria are so precisely designed that any assessor would come to the same evaluation/grade given the same evidence.

Consistent: ensuring inter-tutor and intra-tutor consistency, so that whatever member of the assessment team grades the task and however many assignments an individual grader tackles, the same standards of judgement will apply.

Fair: all students should have an equivalent if not identical chance of achievement.

Inclusive: ensuring that diverse students, whether disabled or not, whatever their background, age, gender, social class, ethnicity, race or sexual orientation should be able to engage with assignments on an equal basis. The assessment of practical skills may require particular consideration.

Manageable: for staff and students in terms of the amount of work required, timing of submission dates and turnaround time. Assessment should be realistic in terms of resources available.

5

Authentic: assessing the intended outcome that is truly representative of the achievement within that context, not a proxy which may be easier to achieve but is not linked appropriately with the learning outcome. Both staff and students should have confidence in the assignment as really getting to the heart of what has been learned.

Testing: ensuring that the required standards of achievement are maintained and are pitched at the right level for the stage of study.

Beyond dispute: it should be transparent to stakeholders how the mark was achieved.

Accompanied by developmental and informative feedback: it should help the student know where to go next and give guidance on growth and improvement.

Motivating: it should engage students and inspire them to engage with the topic.

Efficient: the time spent by staff on marking should be roughly proportionate to the importance of the work within the programme.

In an ideal world, it would be wonderful if practical assessment could also be:

Enjoyable: making it something both markers and students enjoy.

Elegant in its simplicity: so that its execution seems naturally aligned with the programme.

Easy to calculate: avoiding excessive use of manual calculation with its inherent possibilities for human error.

Uncomplicated: avoiding if possible excessively detailed and particularly confusing briefs, complex set-ups and lots of individual assessor actions.

Time-saving: enabling large numbers of individual outputs to be assessed and returned to students quickly and without stress for all involved.

Synoptic: bringing various components of a learning programme together, targeted in a single assignment.

LINKING PRACTICAL LEARNING OUTCOMES TO ASSESSMENT

Well-expressed statements of intended learning outcomes help students to identify their own targets, and work systematically towards demonstrating their achievement of these targets. If we adopt a holistic approach to course design, it should be possible for students (and others) to see very clearly the links between coursework assignments and exam questions and the related intended learning outcomes. Learning outcomes can sometimes be helpful in encouraging the students to see the big picture in relation to their study, so as well as putting them in the course handbook we should consider including reference to them in task and assignment briefs.

However, there can be dangers in being over-specific, and we may wish to exercise caution in encouraging students to believe there is a fail-safe recipe for success contained within the course documentation and the assignment brief. Knight and Yorke argue that:

> Learned dependence is present when the student relies on the teacher to say what has to be done and does not seek to go beyond the boundaries that they believe to be circumscribing the task. The construction of curricula around explicit learning outcomes risks the inadvertent building-in of circumscriptions or, for the 'strategic' student seeking to balance study and part-time employment, a welcome 'limitation' to what they have to do. Formal and informal feedback can be interrogated for what it can tell about what is expected, and can become part of a vicious spiralling-in towards 'playing it safe', basing action on perceptions of the implicit – as well as the explicit – expectations.
>
> (Knight and Yorke 2003: 134)

They further argue that sometimes our apparent exactitude can be misleading for students and colleagues alike. We need to recognise that at HE level assessment will involve an element of specialist evaluation, relying on the judgement of the assessor to make complex decisions using well-honed judgements, and this cannot be short-circuited by close specification of outcomes:

> There is a need to accept that many expected learning outcomes are intrinsically 'fuzzy', even though they may be expressed in apparently precise terms. The apparent precision usually evaporates as teachers and students come to interpret the outcomes for their different

7

purposes. The 'obvious' solution – to seek ever-tighter specifications of the expected outcomes – merely leads into the entangling and disorientating jungle of details.

(Knight and Yorke 2003: 134)

Efforts to make the process transparent can have limited success if assessors are seeking to have cut-and-dried methods of making assessment decisions:

> Some have tried to transform local judgements into universal ones by benchmarking their standards to Bloom's (1956) taxonomy. His taxonomy was not designed to grade responses, but to inform test writing and the design of teaching units. It is arguable that the vision was to develop a tool that would help local actions (Bloom 1956: 1, 2), which is certainly the intention of the recent and much better elaboration (Anderson and Krathwohl, 2001). As often applied, the 1956 taxonomy is open to severe, arguably fatal, philosophical and psychological challenge.
>
> (Anderson and Sosniak, 1994)

We need to recognise the particular complexity and sophistication of the assessment of live and practical skills at higher levels and acknowledge that the process itself is likely to involve an element of idiosyncratic judgement, informed by one's own experience in professional and practical contexts:

> Assessing educational outcomes is not as straightforward as measuring height and weight . . . One must therefore draw inferences about what students know and can do on the basis of what one sees them say, do, or make in a handful of particular situations. What a student knows and what one observes a student doing are not the same thing . . . Assessment users always reason in the presence of uncertainty; as a result the information produced by an assessment is typically incomplete, inconclusive and amenable to more than one explanation.
>
> (Pellegrino *et al.* 2001: 42)

A SAMPLE FRAMEWORK FOR ASSESSING PRACTICAL CAPABILITY

A framework like the one in Figure 1.2 can enable students to undertake assessment once they are reasonably confident of achievement in separate components of an extended assignment.

Date observed	Date rehearsed	Competencies	Ready to be assessed	Date of assessment	Outcome
		1 Can identify. . .			
		2 Can demonstrate. . .			
		3 Can explain. . .			
		4 Can diagnose. . .			
		5 Can record. . .			
		6 Can locate. . .			
		7 Can produce. . .			
		8 Can argue. . .			
		9 Can show. . .			
		10 Can extrapolate. . .			
		11 Can propose cause of. . .			
		12 Can indicate reasons for choosing. . .			

FIGURE 1.2 A framework for assessing practical capability

The language we use in designing practical learning outcomes that link to assessment is crucial (Box 1.2). Sadly, many of those in current use were designed in haste to conform to institutional requirements under time pressure, and many of these continue to be used, unchanged, today. Too often, learning outcomes are expressed in obscure and inaccessible language designed to satisfy validation panels, and then are presented unabridged as part of the course handbooks to students who may find them jargon-ridden and impossibly verbose. When translating practical learning outcomes into assignment briefs and criteria, we have an opportunity to revisit our original intentions and ambitions for student achievement.

Race (2005), Knight and Yorke (2003) and others would counsel strongly against the use of words like 'understand', 'appreciate' and

---

Box 1.2
THE LANGUAGE USED WITHIN PRACTICAL LEARNING OUTCOMES

The verbs used within practical learning outcomes can be really helpful as a first stage in prompting our thinking about what we want to judge and grade. The following list is roughly arranged in order of complexity so that assignment designers can match the task to the level and complexity of the task:

- Demonstrate, show, list, outline, describe
- Design, create, develop, implement, make, plan, construct, articulate, formulate, solve
- Identify, discriminate between, select, sort, choose, prioritise
- Explain, translate, specify, argue, reason, test
- Develop, enable, facilitate, manage
- Challenge, critique, research, design, analyse
- Compare, contrast, judge, evaluate

'know' since it is so difficult to gauge within an assignment the extent to which these have actually been achieved:

> There is uncertainty about what counts as understanding. Side-stepping some important philosophical issues, we suggest that a student who understands something is able to apply it appropriately to a fresh situation (demonstration by far transfer) or to evaluate it (demonstration by analysis). Understanding cannot be judged, then, by evaluating the learner's retention of data or information; rather, assessment tasks would need to have the student *apply* data or information appropriately.
>
> (Knight and Yorke 2003: 48)

Some tips on designing practical learning outcomes:

- **Think ahead to practical assessment right at the beginning of the course design process;** it is much more likely to be constructively aligned if you do, and will allow you to build in opportunities to practice the skill.

Box 1.3
MAKING THE TASK FIT THE OUTCOME

The following tasks have been used in HEIs as replacements for traditional written assignments, to demonstrate the achievement of capability in realistic contexts:

- Undertaking guided information retrieval tasks
- Designing/producing a training/teaching resource
- Writing an annotated bibliography
- Preparing a conference presentation
- Preparing a conference poster
- Writing a magazine article
- Conducting an electronic survey and analysing results
- Writing a one-page digest/short article/feature
- Creating a mind-map
- Doing a risk assessment

- **Write learning outcomes that you can assess practically,** because if the links between the learning outcome and the practical assessment are unclear to you they will be for students and fellow markers as well.
- **Work out what you want students to be able to do by the end of each defined learning element.** You can then use this as guidance in helping you to draft practical assignment briefs.
- **Use your practical learning outcomes as a map to your practical teaching and support programme.** When you want to ensure coverage within the assessment strategy, it will be relatively easy to make the connections.
- **Don't have too many, too lengthy or multiple practical learning outcomes.** There may be associated resource implications and this will also make it difficult for you to design appropriate marking criteria that are easy to cross-reference to the learning outcomes.
- **Consider using (non-constraining) examples ('range statements').** These will give students, particularly those at

11

the beginning of a learning programme, a better idea of the
level of practical skills you are expecting to see from them.

■ **Don't over-specify practice performance standards
and conditions.** It is easy to fall into the trap of constraining
your expectations of student achievement and inhibiting
creativity if you do so.

■ **Test-run your practical learning outcomes and linked
assignments with live participants.** Ask friendly 'guinea
pigs' to advise you whether it is clear what they are expected
to achieve.

■ **Avoid triviality/reductionism in what you are asking
students to do.** There should be an element of challenge in
each assignment and an opportunity for students to achieve at
different levels.

(Adapted from Race 1999)

Chapter 2

Assessing practical skills

The value of formative assessment

It would be unthinkable to assess practical skills without rehearsal and practice opportunities in advance. In many of the areas under discussion in this book, formative feedback is one of the principal means by which students learn and improve. This chapter will concentrate on how we can use formative assessment as part of the developmental process and will argue that, in so doing, we can improve student retention and enhance students' confidence in their live and practical abilities.

THE IMPORTANCE OF FEEDBACK

John Cowan, formerly director of the Open University in Scotland, famously described assessment as the engine that drives learning, to which we would add that feedback is the oil that lubricates the cogs of understanding.

In this chapter we will focus on how formative assessment can maximise learning opportunities for students whose work involves demonstrating practical skills.

AND 'FEED-FORWARD'?

In practice, most feedback comprises not just commentary about what has been done, but suggestions for what can be done next. In particular, advice about how to improve the next element of work can be particularly helpful to students receiving feedback in practical contexts, especially when this advice is received during the progress of the work, so that adjustments can be made in an ongoing manner. It can be worth checking that enough 'feed-forward' is being given, rather than merely feedback on what has already been done.

It is also important to help students themselves to distinguish between feedback and feed-forward, and to look carefully for the latter, regard it as the most useful part, and consciously build upon it as their practical work progresses.

WHAT IS FORMATIVE ASSESSMENT?

This is a highly contested term with no common understanding in the literature. Orsmond *et al.* (2004) have identified from the literature a range of interpretations of the term. Here we will use the following working definition:

> The process used . . . to recognise, and respond to, student learning in order to enhance that learning, *during learning*.
>
> (Cowie and Bell 1999) (our italics)

WHAT'S THE DIFFERENCE BETWEEN FORMATIVE AND SUMMATIVE ASSESSMENT?

Sadler, who has written extensively about the powerful impact that formative assessment can have on achievement, suggests:

> Summative contrasts with formative assessment in that it is concerned with summing up or summarizing the achievement status of a student, and is geared towards reporting at the end of a course of study especially for purposes of certification. It is essentially passive and does not normally have immediate impact on learning, although it often influences decisions which may have profound educational and personal consequences for the student. The primary distinction between formative and summative assessment relates to purpose and effect, not to timing.
>
> (Sadler 1989)

A number of writers argue that 'pure' formative assessment does not include marks and grades, and Sadler concurs with this view:

> A grade therefore may actually be counterproductive for formative purposes. In assessing the quality of a student's work or performance, the teacher must possess a concept of quality appropriate to the task, and be able to judge the student's work in relation to that concept.
>
> (Sadler 1989)

Nevertheless, many assessors feel that for students, particularly those working to demonstrate capability in live and practical skills, some kind of indication of level of achievement is valuable, and that formative assessment is principally a means by which tutors can support the development of their students' understanding and encourage them to progress by providing feedback that is meaningful to the individual.

THE ROLE OF THE TUTOR IN PROVIDING FORMATIVE FEEDBACK

The role of the teacher could broadly be described as working to reduce (but not necessarily eliminate) the rate of error production in trial and error learning, and thereby to make learning more efficient (Sadler 1998).

GETTING STUDENTS TO MAKE USE OF FORMATIVE FEEDBACK

Many students are poor at using feedback constructively. Often they are only interested in the mark (Wotjas 1998), and sometimes they don't even bother to read what we have written. When receiving feedback live, they frequently fail to retain what is said to them, apart from when their own views (or worst fears) of how they have performed are confirmed. Sadler argues that getting a clear picture in mind of the characteristics of high quality work is imperative:

> A key premise is that for students to be able to improve, they must develop the capacity to monitor the quality of their own work during actual production, rather than later on. This in turn requires that students possess an appreciation of what high quality work is, that they have the evaluative skill necessary for them to compare with some objectivity the quality of what they are producing in relation to the higher standard, and that they develop a store of tactics or moves which can be drawn upon to modify their own work.
>
> (Sadler 1989)

We need to find ways to help students make good use of the hard work we put into giving them feedback, to interpret it appropriately, to see how the comments and advice they are given links to what they are doing, and to turn this into improvements in competence and knowledge.

15

Sadler proposes that it is crucial that the student works with the feedback s/he receives in order to internalise the standards that are required:

> The indispensable conditions for improvement are that the student comes to hold a concept of quality roughly similar to that held by the teacher, is able to monitor continuously the quality of what is being produced during the act of production itself, and has a repertoire of alternative moves or strategies from which to draw at any given point. In other words, students have to be able to judge the quality of what they are producing and be able to regulate what they are doing during the doing of it.
>
> (Sadler 1989)

Giving formative feedback is not unproblematic. We can't just assume that students know what to do with the commentary we give them; we need to help them engage with it positively and productively. Sadler further describes:

> the common but puzzling observation that even when teachers provide students with valid and reliable judgments about the quality of their work, improvement does not necessarily follow. Students often show little or no growth or development despite regular, accurate feedback. The concern itself is with whether some learners fail to acquire expertise because of specific deficiencies in the instructional system associated with formative assessment.
>
> (Sadler 1989)

USING FORMATIVE ASSESSMENT TO IMPROVE STUDENT RETENTION

In relatively recent history in UK higher education, high rates of 'wastage' were regarded as a form of quality assurance. 'Look to the right and left of you,' students in their first lecture at university were commonly told, 'and remember only one of you will achieve a degree.' This brutalist approach certainly weeded out the unconfident and those who didn't really think they belonged in higher education anyway, but didn't do a lot for social justice. Today most academics would hold back from such an approach, but residual sentiments of that kind still remain in some pockets of traditionalism. However, nowadays staff are more likely to be deeply concerned to maximise the number of students who successfully complete their awards, not only because it is now a key governmental performance indicator in many countries, the ignoring of which can result in financial penalties, but also because they work in values-driven organisations that genuinely care about students as people, not just as statistics.

Yorke and Longden (2004), who have pioneered research into student retention in the UK, propose a number of reasons for student non-completion. Among these, the lack of formative assessment ranks highly, especially in the early stages of a programme of learning. If students haven't a clue about how they are doing, a negative mindset can easily develop, leading to a downward spiral and ultimate drop out.

SO WHAT DO YOU EXPECT?

A number of studies have suggested that a key issue lies around the management of expectations of students about what studying at degree level implies. For many undergraduate students on degree courses, particularly those studying part-time, balancing paid work, caring responsibilities and studying can lead to a corner-cutting approach in which only essential tasks are completed. This means in essence that they only do assessed work, and only this if there are heavy penalties for non-completion. Bowl reported one of the students in her study saying:

> If 25 per cent of your marks is from reading, you've got to try and show that, even if you haven't read. I'm not going to sit there and read a chapter, and I'm certainly not going to read a book. But I'll read little paragraphs that I think are relevant to what I'm writing, and it's got me through, and my marks have been fine. But I can't read. If I read too much, it goes over my head. If I'm writing some-thing, I know what I want to say and I need something to back me up . . . then I will find something in a book that goes with that. I'm not going to try to take in the whole book just for one little bit. I have my book next to me and then I can pick out the bits. (Jenny, full-time community and youth work student).
>
> (Bowl 2003: 89)

Students in Bowl's study experienced worrying levels of lack of clarity about what is expected of them, despite having been given plenty of advice in course documentation:

17

The hardship was not understanding. When they give you an assignment and say it was on this handout. But my difficulty is not understanding what to do at first. And if you don't read, you're not going to learn certain things. So I suppose that's to do with me . . . it's reading as well as putting what you read into your essay. You can read it and understand it. I can read and understand it, but then you have to incorporate it into your own words. But in the words they want you to say it in, not just: She said this, and this is the way it should be. The words, the proper language. Maybe it's because I have difficulty pronouncing certain words. I avoid using them as they're not familiar to me. When I'm writing, I find that because I'm not familiar with those words, it's hard to write them . . . I haven't really gone into it, because I don't want them to say, you're not supposed to be on this course, or anything like that. I've come too far now for them to say that, so I don't like raising the issue. (Helen, brought up in Jamaica).

(Bowl 2003: 90)

When assessing students' live and practical skills, then, we need to be very clear about specifying the types of academic activity we expect of students, who may be primarily involved in a range of practical tasks and who may have specifically chosen a course of study because they thought it would involve little in the way of traditional academic work. We should clarify the extent to which they must demonstrate underpinning knowledge within assignments, and how best they can do this, as well as how to provide evidence for these theoretical sub-structures.

THE IMPORTANCE OF FORMATIVE ASSESSMENT IN FOSTERING ACADEMIC SKILLS

We are used to hearing much about the problems students experience with getting inside the academic discourse and discovering how best to undertake academic *writing* in ways that often don't come naturally to second-chance or late-achieving students. However, there seems to be a real crisis about *reading* among students, and one of the problems emerging about formative assessment is the danger that those very students who are feeling swamped by all the reading required of them to undertake HE courses will be the ones who find themselves directed towards yet more reading of formative feedback, whether this is tutor- or peer-initiated.

In the context of widening participation, perhaps we need to reconsider *our* expectations about the amount of reading we require of our students. When less than 10 per cent of the 18–30 population participated in higher education, it may have been reasonable to expect that our students would be likely to have well-developed skills relating to academic reading. With approaching 50 per cent of the 18–30 population in higher education, it should not surprise us that a significant proportion of our students have not attained this level of expertise in reading for academic purposes by the time they come to study with us. Can we *train* all these students to the necessary extent? Or should we perhaps be considering *reducing* our expectations regarding academic reading, and focusing on the *quality* of reading rather than the *quantity or breadth* or reading?

 Case study 2.1

There is no doubt that putting effort and resources into helping students understand what is required of them pays dividends. Sambell and Hubbard (2004) are currently exploring how best to redesign assessment methods to enhance formative assessment opportunities for non-traditional students, especially in the first year of undergraduate study. They are particularly investigating non-traditional students' perspectives of low-stakes assessment strategies when they are introduced into the early stages of their course, as a means of easing their transition to university study.

Students undertake a module on 'Writing at University' which is delivered through four interactive lead lectures. They are required to complete a workbook which gives them plenty of rehearsal and review opportunities to help them develop critical and reflective skills in reading and writing. Many of the students in this study found the higher education context baffling and alien, and overall the study showed that they found the approach very helpful in helping them understand what was required of them. For example, one student cited in the study said: 'It's quite a new way of writing for me and it's certainly new to think about it from a marker's point of view. It was really helpful seeing how you could write about these things and what looks good and less good' (Sambell and Hubbard 2004: 36).

19

SURVIVING KNOCK-BACKS: THE CONFIDENCE ISSUE

Students from non-traditional academic backgrounds are likely to find their confidence level is further undermined if their belief in their own abilities to succeed is undermined by conceptions about themselves which have made it difficult for them to achieve academically in the past.

Clegg (2002), citing Dweck (2000), argues that there is a high correlation between self-concept and achievement, and this depends on whether students see their capabilities as being set in stone or malleable through hard work and strategic approaches. They discuss two positions that students can adopt in regard to their own abilities, first that intelligence is fixed (an entity theory of intelligence, as evidenced by IQ scores) and that there is very little they can do to improve themselves, and second that ability is malleable, and that hard work can lead to high achievement (an incremental theory of intelligence):

> The personal commitment an individual makes to a theory of intelligence is indicative of their self perception. Students who subscribe to an entity theory of intelligence believe that failure is the final point, the outcome of their achievements. They need 'a diet of easy successes' (Dweck, 2000:15) to confirm their ability and are fearful of learning goals as this involves an element of risk and personal failure. Assessment for these students is an all-encompassing activity that defines them as people. If they fail at the task, they *are* failures. Challenges are a threat to self-esteem as it is through being seen to be successful that these students define themselves. . .Perhaps predictably, those students who believe that intelligence is incremental have little or no fear of failure. A typical response from such a student is 'The harder it gets, the harder I need to try'. These students do not see failure as an indictment of themselves and [can] separate their self-image from their academic achievement. When faced with a challenge, these students are more likely to continue in the face of adversity because they have nothing to prove.
>
> (Clegg 2002: 176)

Such self-beliefs are remarkably persistent and can interfere powerfully in how a student responds to negative comments in feedback from tutors:

20

Blaming oneself for failure indicates an incremental theory of intelligence. Students believe they could have done something to avoid failure and will try harder next time . . . In other words, students choose how they interpret feedback and failure so as to lessen the emotional damage. Students deny the validity of teacher, peer and professional judgement if it disagrees with their own self concept.

(Clegg 2002: 177)

SO WHAT'S TO BE DONE?

Yorke (*op cit*) provides us with confidence that we can actually make a difference to the dismal picture of drop-out and perceptions of failure:

Whereas a higher education institution can not do much about students' background circumstances, it is probable that there is more academic failure in UK higher education than there should be. There seems to be scope in institutions for improving the ways in which they support students' learning – and hence for reducing the incidence of academic failure. In the end, this comes down to an orientation towards the enhancement of the quality of the student experience.

(Yorke and Longden 2004: 39)

There is a case to be made for HEIs to consider spending considerable time and resources on students undertaking their first programmes of study to help them understand the purposes of formative feedback and how their own self-beliefs can impact on the ways they receive it. Inevitably this would eat into available time for content delivery, which academic staff no doubt would be unwilling to see slimmed down, but if we are serious about retaining students as a key means of survival in an increasingly competitive world, then tough decisions might have to be made.

Yorke and Longden suggest that rather than compliance with requirements for externally imposed performance indicators, it may be necessary to redefine failure as a student's informed choice. All students, of whatever age, have the right to make decisions about their experiences of 'failure' on any course and to redefine their withdrawal in ways that enable them to rationalise the experience so that it is as positive as possible.

CONCLUSIONS

Boud (1995) argues that 'Students can avoid bad teaching: they can't avoid bad assessment.' Many would argue that concentrating on giving students detailed and developmental formative feedback is the single most useful thing we can do for them, particularly those who have struggled to achieve entry to higher education. To do so may require considerable re-engineering not just of our assessment processes but also of curriculum design as a whole if we are to move from considering delivering content to be the most important thing we do.

Some suggestions on using formative feedback to enhance learning when assessing live and practical skills:

- **Plan to maximise the impact of formative feedback.** Consider how you can make space to spend extra time helping students to understand the importance of feedback in the development of practical skills and the value of spending some time after receiving back work to learn from the experience.

- **Provide opportunities for students to respond to your feedback.** This can either be done live or by giving students a follow-up task, for example when they are asked to provide a list of action points stemming from the assignment or to indicate in a future task how they have used the feedback as feed-forward to improve their next piece of work.

- **Think about the means by which you deliver feedback.** This can be vital in determining how much notice students take of what you say. The most useful feedback in developing practical skills can often take the form of a demonstration of the practical skill. Ideally, giving feedback should be as personal as possible, with opportunities for dialogue individually or collectively.

- **Ensure that students receiving oral feedback have a means of recording this.** Either require them to take notes or use an audiotape so that they can reconsider what has been said, after the actual event, recollecting in tranquillity what they have heard in the heat of the moment of an assessment.

- **Get work back to students really fast in the early stages of a programme.** Many universities have standard guidelines on how quickly to do this (normally 2–4 weeks). Consider whether it is possible to do this even faster, or in an even more personal way – such as a quick phone call or email as soon as marking is complete, perhaps especially targeted at students in groups known to be at risk of dropping out.

- **Consider giving them 'instant feedback' immediately after demonstration/submission.** For example, a page or two of comments responding to 'frequently occurring problems', or illustrative details along the lines 'good practice would include . . . ' can give students some useful feedback while their work is still fresh in their minds, and can keep them going until they receive the detailed and individual feedback on their own attempts in due course. There could, however, be problems where a submission date was 'slack', for example unwanted collusion between prompt students who gained this feedback straight away and students who were already late in submitting their assignments.

- **Explore further the uses of computer-assisted formative assessment.** While computer-assisted assessment (CAA) is used in some contexts summatively, many would argue that it is most powerfully used to support formative feedback, especially where automatically generated by email. Students seem to really like having the chance to find out how they are doing, and attempt tests several times in an environment where no one else is watching how they do. Another benefit is that CAA systems allow you to monitor what is going on across a cohort, enabling you to concentrate your energies either on students who are repeatedly doing badly or those who are not engaging at all in the activity.

- **Provide extra 'scaffolding' for students at risk of failure.** Intensive extra help could be offered in the early stages of programmes and then be progressively removed as students became more independent and confident in their own practical abilities.

- **Review the advice given to students to help them understand what is required of them in terms of writing.** Work with them to understand the various academic discourses that are employed within your HEI, and help them to understand when writing needs to be personal and based on individual experience, such as in a reflective log, and when it needs to be formal and using academic conventions like passive voice and third person, as in written reports and essays.

23

- **Consider carefully the advice students are given on different kinds of approaches needed for reading.** These might include reading for pleasure, for information, for understanding or reading around a topic. Students who come new to HE learning are likely to need advice on becoming active readers with a pen and *Post-its* in hand, rather than passive readers, fitting the task in alongside television and other noisy distractions.

- **Ensure that the language used when giving feedback to students avoids destructive criticism of the person rather than assessing the work.** Boud (1995) talks about the disadvantages of using 'final language', that is, language that is judgemental to the point of leaving students nowhere to go. Words like 'appalling', 'disastrous' and 'incompetent' fall into this category, but so do words like 'incomparable' and 'unimprovable' if they don't help outstanding students to develop ipsatively also.

- **Consider providing opportunities for resubmissions of work as part of a planned programme.** Students often feel they could do better work once they have seen the formative feedback and would like the chance to have another go. Particularly in the early stages of a programme, consider offering them the chance to use formative feedback productively. Feedback often involves a change of orientation, not just the remediation of errors.

- **Think about ways of getting students to give each other formative feedback.** Involve students in their own and each other's assessment. Reflection is not a luxury; it is the best means available to help them really get inside the criteria and understand the often hidden 'rules of the game'. In particular, asking students to review each other's practical work prior to submission can be really helpful for all students, but particularly those who lack confidence about what kinds of things are expected of them.

Chapter 3

Ensuring equivalence of experience for disabled students

This chapter considers how we can improve good practice in assessing the practical and live skills of disabled students, and evaluating students' achievements fairly. This chapter draws heavily on ideas discussed at the UK Higher Education Funding Council for England funded National Disability Team annual conference in April 2005. In the UK we have particular incentives to work towards inclusive assessment practice for disabled students, since following the Special Educational Needs and Disabilities Act (SENDA) 2001 we have a legal obligation to ensure that no student is discriminated against on the grounds of special educational needs or disability. This includes not just mobility, hearing and visual impairments, but also mental health difficulties, dyslexia and hidden impairments such as diabetes, asthma, heart disease and other serious illnesses.

In exploring how best to be inclusive, many UK HEIs have drawn on good practice elsewhere, notably Australia, New Zealand, Canada and the US, and have aimed to implement approaches that not only avoid discriminatory behaviour but also demonstrate good practice for all students, not just disabled ones. Inclusive practice enriches the experience of all who study and work at university.

Assessment cultures are often among the most conservative aspects of pedagogic design to tackle inclusivity, since assessment plays such a pivotal part in the student learning experience. At an institutional level, inclusive assessment practice needs to be tackled systematically. This is likely to mean, for example, requiring all staff to participate in mandatory staff development on inclusive assessment practice. This might well include:

- training for senior managers so they can steer institutional policy appropriately;

- inclusive assessment practice in induction for academic and learning support staff as well as in postgraduate certificates in higher education practice;
- developing institutional handbooks setting out expectations and examples of good practice for both staff and students. HEIs need to ensure that all policy/strategy documents on inclusive practice are achieved, by wide consultation and discussion involving frontline assessors who can input their real experiences of working with disabled students.

The vocabulary of disability/inclusivity, based on the medical model, traditionally uses terms like 'help', 'support', 'advice', 'deficit', 'needs' and 'disclosure', as if disability is something shameful. The focus of recent legislation in the UK is on positive anticipatory duty to make practice inclusive. We will need therefore to impact-assess every new programme at validation to ensure that we are not making life unnecessarily difficult for disabled students. It is not cost-effective or sensible to provide alternatives for individual students in an ad hoc, last minute way. It is far better to ensure that the thinking about alternatives is done at the point of curriculum design, which avoids disabled students feeling marked out or marginalised unnecessarily by being treated differently.

It is also valuable to build into an institutional learning and teaching strategy the requirement that course teams consider alternative assessments for disabled students at the approval and re-approval stage, rather than making special one-off arrangements for individuals at the last moment. Special arrangements for disabled students are normally put in place nowadays for formal examinations, but too often are forgotten about for in-class tests, coursework and assessment of practical work and performances. Many would argue that it's not difficult to think up alternative assessment methods but the real difficulty lies in ensuring that they are equivalent and that standards are assured. There will always be a small number of students who will still need idiosyncratic adjustments to be made but we can avoid the majority of special arrangements by thinking ahead. When it comes to professional courses that result in a licence to practice, HEIs and professional bodies, under amendments to the Disability Discrimination Act part 2, have a duty of care to ensure that all graduates with professional qualifications are able to demonstrate such fitness to practice, but this should not be used as an excuse to do nothing. A way forward here could be to involve disabled and other students in helping to design a variety of alternatives to traditional forms, methods and approaches to assessment.

Some general tips on the design of an inclusive approach to assessing live and practical skills are:

- **Build in reasonable adjustments to assessment arrangements at the course design and re-approval stage.** These are likely to be the most efficient and effective points at which to consider alternatives, rather than waiting for problems to present themselves at the last minute.
- **Undertake a needs analysis for assessment requirements as soon as students are involved.** This will maximise the time available for additional idiosyncratic adjustments to be made for students whose needs had not been foreseen.
- **Make best use of university disability officers and other informed colleagues to build a knowledge base of the needs of disabled students.** There is considerable expertise within a university, but this is not always sufficiently coordinated to be highly effective at an institutional level.
- **Make use of disabled students to advise on inclusive assessment practice.** The likelihood is that the majority of disabled students already have successful study strategies prior to coming to university and they will also know where pitfalls and problems are likely to arise in assignments for students with similar impairments to their own. Some universities have established advisory panels of disabled students to work with staff to promote inclusive pedagogic practice.
- **Consider abolishing formal unseen time-constrained exams.** You are likely to want to use vivas, take-away papers, portfolios and other forms of assessment anyway for assessing live and practical skills but sometimes course teams feel compelled to include some exams to satisfy institutional requirements and external assessors. Your course design process should be seeking fit-for-purpose assessment methods that constructively align with your learning outcomes. These do not necessarily include traditional exams.
- **Consider from the outset the health and safety requirements of disabled students who are to be engaged in practicals and field trips.** Considerable work has been done in this area by the University of Gloucestershire (see *Enhancing the quality and outcomes of disabled students' learning*

27

in higher education, http://www.glos.ac.uk/schools/education/tirp/the-team.cfm).

■ **Learn from good practice elsewhere.** There is a need to develop a repository of learning from previous and current adjustments so you build expertise across the department/institution.

ASSESSING DYSLEXIC STUDENTS' LIVE AND PRACTICAL SKILLS

In some programmes involving skills and practice, disabled students make up a significant minority of the cohort. For example, the proportion of disabled students on some courses, including specialist art and design courses, can be as high as 40 per cent, with the most common disability being dyslexia. This is unsurprising since bright students with difficulties in traditional academic skills are likely to seek out subjects for study where their intelligence and capabilities can be best demonstrated, without their grades being diminished by an inordinate focus on reading and writing abilities.

Students with dyslexia make up the vast majority of students who describe themselves as disabled at UK HEIs, for example, at the University of Gloucestershire more than 60 per cent of those who declare themselves to be disabled are dyslexic. Features of dyslexia can include poor and slow hand writing, mixed spelling ability, slow reading, structural and grammatical difficulties in writing, short-term memory problems and disorganisation. However, dyslexic students often excel at problem solving, conceptualisation and conveying/understanding information in visual formats, and frequently are highly intelligent. Students with dyslexia are often over-represented among mature students who may not have succeeded in HE earlier in their lives due to their unacknowledged (by self or others) impairment.

 Case study 3.1

SPACE (Staff–Student Partnership for Assessment Change and Evaluation) is a three-year HEFCE funded project based at the University of Plymouth which is developing and promoting alternative forms of assessment as a way of facilitating a more inclusive approach to assessment. They have found that

71 per cent of the 100 disabled students they surveyed were in receipt of special examination arrangements. Of these, 67 per cent of the disabled students surveyed received extra time to complete work. The SPACE team argue that this may not necessarily be the best way of supporting disabled students undertaking assessment and are developing an inclusive assessment toolkit.

Guidelines developed by SPACE suggest, for example, involving students themselves in designing special examination arrangements and offering alternatives to traditional dissertations, including video and oral assessments. Details of the SPACE project can be accessed at http://www.space.ac.uk/assess.php.

Reasonable adjustments for assessing skills and practice for students with dyslexia include:

- **Try to separate the assessment of the content from the assessment of the expression of language.** This will allow tutors to judge the extent to which the student has met the whole range of learning outcomes.
- **When marking students with dyslexia, decide on the extent to which spelling/grammar/logical ordering should impact on the marks given.** Dyslexic students are in some cases repeatedly penalised for spelling, grammar and ordering errors in their written work. Assessors need to decide the extent to which these aspects are important in each assignment, and what weighting should accordingly be given.
- **Decide on the extent to which these aspects of work should be the subject of formative feedback and how it will impact on summative grades.** This will depend substantially on the nature, level, content and context of the assignment and how much accuracy and presentation are integral to learning outcomes. They would be more important, for example, on a journalism course than on a software design course.
- **Provide printed instructions for all assignments in advance.** This can be really helpful for students who have difficulty with self-organisation.
- **Check with individual students which print fonts, sizes and paper colours are easiest for them to handle.**

29

This can be a way of making it much easier for affected students to make sense of the assignment briefings.

■ **Find out whether affected students may work best on-screen rather than on paper.** This can, for example, allow them to use software as they compose their answers so that they can hear what they have written, often alerting them to changes they need to make to their phrasing and grammar.

■ **Consider the suitability of mind maps and other alternatives to written communication when students are being assessed on how well they can organise ideas.** Dyslexic students can often think faster than they are able to present ideas in conventional written formats.

■ **In making tutor comments on students' work, pay particular attention to the legibility of your own writing.** It may be a tough task for many students to make out what you are trying to say if you scrawl, and those with particular issues with writing may simply give up trying. You might wish to consider using typescript for all comments. You should also make your comments succinct and explicit.

■ **Remember that different dyslexic students will be helped by different adjustments.** Ask individual students about what fonts, colours and formats are most helpful to them, and seek specialist advice where necessary.

ASSESSING THE SKILLS AND PRACTICE OF STUDENTS WITH VISUAL IMPAIRMENTS

Higher education relies heavily on reading and writing as the key elements of academic transactions, even on courses that involve a high level of live and practical skills, where logocentric work is seen as inextricably linked to the assurance of quality in many areas. Inevitably this is likely to provide considerable challenges for visually impaired students. Work undertaken by HEFCE funded projects suggests that we need to develop assessment responses that are equitable by building empirical data on what accommodations work best for students with visual impairments.

Some reasonable adjustments for assessing students with visual impairments include:

■ **Ensure that written materials are available in other media.** Take advice on what an individual student needs: not all students need or like to use large fonts, for example. Only about 10 per cent of blind students are Braille readers and so it is sometimes just a case of sending the information to students electronically in order that their software can 'read' the material to them. You might also wish to seek specialist support in the production of 'tactile diagrams' which can bring alive some materials for students with visual impairments.

■ **Reduce the length of time it may take to make accessible materials available.** Students report they sometimes have to wait a long time to receive materials in alternative formats, since this is not always thought out by staff at the course development process. Too often this provision is left until the last minute, or post hoc, which is unacceptable in cases where staff knew about the presence of students with visual impairments from the outset. Tutors must allow plenty of time for preparation of reading lists to ensure sufficient time for conversion into alternative formats.

■ **Make it easier for students to find what they need in order to attempt the assignment.** Students with visual impairments can have difficulty accessing learning resources in libraries and resource centres which may be physically dispersed around the university.

■ **Set inclusive assignment briefs.** When setting group assignments that rely on visual case studies, images or other materials that are not accessible to visually impaired students, consider how you and fellow students can make them part of the process.

■ **Help to make it possible for students readily to transcribe or otherwise record field notes and experimental write-ups.** Remember it may take them extra time, and seek their advice on what assistance they need.

ASSESSING STUDENTS WITH MENTAL HEALTH DIFFICULTIES

This is an extremely complex area which HEIs have only started addressing relatively recently. Clegg (2002) and others have argued that assessment activities can have a seriously deleterious effect on students with mental health problems and anecdotally we know that exam and assignment stress can be the last straw that pushes students into episodes of mental ill-health.

It is also being increasingly recognised that mental health issues frequently surface for the first time for people in the age range 18–25, which is precisely when many students are entering HE for the first time. Research by projects supported by the National Disability Team also shows strong links between mental health issues and excessive use of alcohol and drugs. For example, both cannabis and alcohol are recognised as common if dysfunctional coping strategies by people dealing with depression, but these can in turn exacerbate the original problems and their use arouses little sympathy from tutors who often only see the presenting problem.

A range of undiagnosed mental health conditions can lead to inability to undertake assignment organisation, difficulties in application and attendance problems that we know are linked to student drop-out. Too often this is tackled on a crisis intervention basis.

The most commonly used adjustment for all disabled students in written assignments is the allowance of extra time for completion of the work. For many students with mental health issues, this can only make things worse. Students with obsessive compulsive behaviour, for example, are unlikely to find the extra time helpful.

Some reasonable adjustments when assessing students experiencing anxiety and other mental health issues in live and practical assignments include:

- **Consider offering a 'stop the clock' facility in time-constrained assessments, such as practical examinations or demonstrations, for students with mental health difficulties.** For those students with anxiety, just having this potential often means they don't need to use the facility since they are less anxious.
- **Offer a holistic approach to the student experience.** Some HEIs are finding that exploring the links between health, diet, exercise and mental health disorders can pay dividends. For example, the University of Northumbria is investigating the benefits of exercise programmes for such students.
- **Provide advance organisers, which help students map out their responsibilities and plan to meet deadlines, for all students in the early stages of HE programmes.** This may set patterns of behaviour that help anxious students feel comfortable about hand-in dates and organise their work

accordingly. It may also have the side benefit of ensuring that teaching staff are less likely unknowingly to set multiple deadlines for students just starting to organise their study lives, potentially for the first time.

- **Consider offering practical assignments with staged completion times and dates.** By completing work in incremental stages, students are less likely to experience the 'ground-rush' effect where everything seems to be coming towards them at an alarming rate.

- **Think about simplifying the structure of practical tests.** Setting fewer yet equally demanding tasks or questions in tests may help students who feel anxious when faced with multiple requirements in a tightly curtailed time-period.

- **Start practical assessment at the beginning of the day or after a break.** The Royal Northern College of Music have found that this can have benefits in combating performance anxiety. Students who are waiting around can get increasingly nervous as the time for their assignment looms ever nearer.

- **Provide practical assignments in two or more parts.** This can enable anxious students to concentrate on one item at a time and to focus their energies appropriately.

- **Enable students with anxiety to familiarise themselves with the assessment context in advance.** For example, enabling students to visit the studio, concert hall or exam room where a practical or live assessment will take place prior to the occasion can be reassuring for some students who otherwise might find themselves disorientated by an unfamiliar context. In some cases it might be possible to offer them the facility of undertaking the assignment in their own home, or with music in the background.

- **Use a known invigilator.** If a familiar person is managing the exam invigilation or demonstration process, this can be very helpful for students with anxiety.

- **Offer an alternative demonstration or presentation timing.** For example, indicate an eight-hour period in which a student can demonstrate their skills, which will take up five hours of work, and let the student decide when to start and finish.

- **Provide mentors to help students understand how the system works.** For example, mentors have been found to be

33

helpful at Oxford University to students with Asperger's Syndrome by helping them to structure their studies appropriately. These can be provided through disability support funds in the UK under SENDA legislation.

- **For students whose behaviour can be disconcerting to others, provide behavioural learning plans.**
Inappropriate behaviour can lead to disciplinary proceedings, yet autistic students, for example, can be unaware of the impact of their behaviour on others. It can also impact negatively on assessed group work. At the University of Tasmania they have successfully used agreed behaviour plans which create and clarify expectations.

ASSESSING HEARING IMPAIRED STUDENTS

In contexts where the majority of assessment is written, it might be assumed that students with hearing impairments would not be disadvantaged. However, many such students have British Sign Language (BSL) or its equivalent as their first language and may therefore be disadvantaged by unfamiliarity with specialist vocabularies/jargon, and their lesser fluency.

In assessing live and practical skills, assessment of hearing impaired students is likely to present additional challenges for HEIs where provision in alternative formats (for example BSL), signing in oral assessments and presentations, captioning on tests using video and other adjustments may be required.

There is nothing more important than to ask each hearing impaired student about their own knowledge of how their impairment may impact on typical assessment processes and contexts. Such students know a great deal about any particular difficulties they experience, and can often indicate straightforward ways in which the assessment can be adjusted to cater for their needs, without compromising standards.

 Case study 3.2

Ravinder, a student with a hearing impairment, was studying a first year systems analysis module which involved observing a ten-minute film of someone at work in a commercial environment and making observation notes (an essential systems analysis skill). Ravinder asked whether the film could be provided in VHS format and explained that, although she could not hear the film when played on her PC, the capacity for higher volume on her television enabled her to hear and complete the assessment.

Some tips for assessing students with hearing impairments:

- **Be aware that students whose first language is British Sign Language may not write standard English fluently.** The kinds of adjustments that are made for the written work of dyslexics or those writing in a second language should be applied in these instances.
- **When assessing students in the lab or other practical context, remember that auditory signals will not be available to students with hearing-impairments.** This applies, for example, when students are dissolving crystals and might not be able to hear when these stop crunching in the beaker, or when students are using equipment that beeps at key points.
- **When giving instructions for assessed live and practical work in the studio, workplace or other learning context, avoid moving about too much or standing in ill-lit areas.** Lip-reading students may be prevented from understanding what you are saying if they can't see you clearly at all times.
- **If the room in which the assessed practical is taking place has a hearing loop, always use a voice microphone if available, even if you have a loud, clear voice.** There may be students who need amplification to pick up what you are saying, particularly if there is a lot of background noise.
- **Encourage fellow students to speak up.** Students on the whole are extremely supportive of disabled students but may need reminding of simple things that can help their peers, like facing the student with hearing impairment when addressing the group. Ideally, let the student concerned identify for fellow students what is most helpful behaviour.
- **When responding to fellow students, for example in group critiques, wherever possible repeat their**

comments, as you would in lectures. This maximises the chances of students with hearing impairments having access to the shared conversation and commentary.

- **Make any reasonable adjustments necessary in assessed presentations.** For example, if a student with a hearing impairment is part of a peer assessment team for an assessed presentation, encourage the presenter to provide a text in advance, use amplification and/or use a signer.
- **Explore the uses of assistive technologies that can quickly turn voice into readable text on a screen during practical assignments.** In the UK, TechDis (www.TechDis.ac.uk) is a national resource advising HE and FE practitioners on a wide range of assistive technologies for disabled students.

ASSESSING THE SKILLS AND PRACTICE OF DISABLED POSTGRADUATE STUDENTS

Research study for postgraduate students can be lonely and isolating, but even more so for disabled postgraduates, who may no longer have access to the support strategies they used effectively through their undergraduate years.

Extended writing tasks for disabled students, with the need to keep multiple, complex ideas in mind simultaneously, can be particularly hard for students with particular impairments including visual impairments and dyslexia, as can the requirement for excellent self-organisation skills and high volumes of reading. Research at Newcastle University (Farrer 2006) shows that while dyslexic students are now proving successful on many undergraduate programmes, there is a huge drop in the number of dyslexic people going on to do research degrees.

Inclusivity needs to be considered from the very beginning of the process: approvals processes for postgraduate study currently tend to focus on content and design rather than accessibility, and this may lead to artificial expectations on both sides. Questions need to be asked by all parties at the outset about how the research study will enable a positive experience for a disabled student.

Extended writing can be physically painful for students with, for example, arthritis, and can make substantial demands on students who use British Sign Language as their first language. Specialist discourses/language requirements can be problematic for such students, too, who are already working in a second language when they use academic English. The whole nature of study also tends to change at this level, with the extent of direction and guidance diminishing sharply. Some postgraduate supervisors have very limited views of what kinds of support to give to postgraduates, with a model of supervision based on apprenticeship and an expectation that students should be independent self-starters. This can cause difficulties for students with poor self-organisation skills.

Additionally, some students may interpret the lack of positive formative feedback they get at this level as negative feedback, and may find that discouraging.

Organisationally there may be issues too: regulations about the length of time taken to complete research degrees can actually make the situation worse for disabled students, who can be disadvantaged by institutions keen to ensure students complete by target dates. Extensions can sometimes be refused for these reasons. Furthermore, vivas may offer particular challenges for students with impairments, especially those related to performance anxiety.

Some reasonable adjustments for postgraduate students:

- **Provide realistic rehearsal opportunities for vivas.** These should mirror as closely as possible what students should expect, with authentic taxing questions and the right number of people asking them in (ideally) the actual room where the viva will take place.
- **Encourage postgraduate students to keep supervisors informed about their progress, and how their impairments may be impacting on their work.** This can ensure that where reasonable adjustments to (for example) deadlines or meeting dates need to be made, there is time to make such adjustments.
- **Clarify what is expected from the outset.** This is just as necessary at postgraduate level as it is at undergraduate level, but supervisors often have high expectations of their postgraduates' ability to anticipate what is expected of them.

Chapter 4

Assessing diverse students fairly

Many nations have powerful legislative and ethical drivers to compel us to ensure that students are treated equally with no discrimination on the basis of age, gender, disability, ethnic background, race, culture, religion, sexual orientation or political beliefs. Carrying this forward into assessment in HE can be a very tall order because, despite good intentions, we are all products of our own contexts and may not always be aware of our own discriminatory behaviour. This chapter draws on international good practice and offers some discussion of how best to assess the practical and live skills of diverse students.

ANONYMITY

Generally it is accepted that to avoid bias in assessment, it is better to assess anonymously. Well-documented examples show that discrimination by gender or ethnicity is not uncommon when markers know the identity of those submitting written work, hence the move towards anonymous marking in that domain. However, it is usually just about impossible to assess live and practical skills anonymously. This means that the normal safeguards we have in place to ensure that our own inherent biases and predilections do not impact on our assessment practices cannot always kick in. We need therefore to be doubly vigilant to ensure that we are being fair and giving each student an equivalent if not identical experience.

ORGANISING ASSESSED GROUP WORK

In many programmes involving live and practical skills, students are expected to work and be assessed in groups. One area in which poor practice can emerge is in selecting the make-up of groups, and sensitivity will need to be exercised when working out group composition. If students self-select their groups, it is possible for those perceived by the majority as outsiders to be left out or marginalised in groups of their own. Sometimes minority students themselves will seek to form groups comprising only students from the same ethnic or racial group as themselves. This may be beneficial to students whose first language is different from the dominant one, since they may have developed very effective mutual support mechanisms, which may be compromised if they are forcibly split up. However, there are likely to be substantial benefits in getting diverse students to work together in groups, to break down some of the barriers that might otherwise be reinforced.

 Case study 4.1

On an engineering programme a cohort of about 60 home students were joined in the second year by around 30 students recruited from a nation on the other side of the world. A well-meaning but misguided tutor, when trying to get them to work in mixed groups of three, insisted that each group contain two home students and one newcomer. The results were very unsatisfactory as the home students resented what they saw as social engineering and the newly arrived international students felt cut off, unwelcome and isolated. In subsequent years the tutor learned from her mistakes and asked each student to identify one other student with whom they would like to work, and then formed groups of six students with a good mix of home and international students. This worked much better.

MANAGING PEER ASSESSMENT OF SKILLS AND PRACTICE

Peer assessment is well-established in many nations, but is less so in others. Indeed, some students may feel completely baffled by the concept of anyone other than their tutor marking their skills development. It is particularly important, therefore, that tutors provide ample briefing and discussion opportunities prior to any live peer assessment.

It may be easiest to introduce inter-peer group assessment, where groups of students collectively or individually assess other groups of students prior to the implementation of intra-peer group assessment, where students are expected, for example, to assess the contributions of other students within their own working groups. In each case, discussion and clarification of criteria and the range of acceptable evidence of the achievement of these criteria is necessary in advance.

When students are assessing one another's tasks, it is especially important that they understand the need to avoid bias (Box 4.1). A number of HEIs have reported that it can be difficult to prevent derogatory or inappropriately negative comments about students from other

---

Box 4.1
AVOIDING BIAS IN ASSESSMENTS

The following trigger comments could be used as part of an exercise to get students thinking about avoiding cultural, sexual or other bias in practical assessment by really focusing on the criteria. You might wish to ask students to discuss what each of the following comments says about the assessor and the person being assessed.

'I couldn't make out a word she was saying because her accent was so strong, so I rated her poorly.'

'I gave him low marks in the presentation because he looked so scruffy. Where I come from, we make an effort to dress smartly for uni, and I think it shows little respect for us that he fails to wear tidy clothes when addressing us.'

'Dated and deadly dull, harping back to the old days when he was a lad. I got nothing from his talk.'

'I didn't really notice what he was saying, but he looked so fit I gave him a good grade.'

'I expect someone giving a good presentation to make eye contact with the audience, but hers never lifted from the floor.'

'She had a very common voice, which made it difficult to take seriously her rationale for her work.'

'The content of his presentation was OK and he was pretty slick, but he was such an arrogant youngster, I downgraded his mark for being so smug.'

'We thought he was so brave doing his presentation despite his stutter that we all gave him a good mark.'

---

cultures and backgrounds in, for example, assessed presentations. In-class exercises as part of the briefings for peer assessment could be valuable in providing opportunities to clarify institutional expectations about anti-discriminatory behaviour between students.

In group skills presentations, students may find it difficult to hear or understand what one another is saying: it might be helpful therefore to encourage them to provide outline notes, annotated diagrams or hand-outs to aid mutual comprehension.

Home students should also be encouraged to consider the extent to which colloquialisms and slang should be used, since these kinds of expressions can marginalise, alienate or confuse students from a different cultural context.

Jokes can also be problematic. For example, in the English language many jokes are based on wordplay, puns and double entendres which do not always translate easily. Nothing makes one feel like an outsider more than failing to see the joke that everyone else is laughing at, and in these instances it is all too easy to assume that the joke is on you.

DIVERSE ASSESSMENT PRACTICE

Assessment is commonly thought to be universal across higher education internationally, but innumerable and sometimes conflicting assessment cultures exist side by side in neighbouring nations. Assessment strate-gies that are implemented in different nations reflect the value systems of those countries, and problems can arise when students find them-selves in contexts where they don't know the rules of the game. Assess-ment is not a neutral area and good inclusive practice suggests the need to provide sometimes quite extensive guidance for students and staff so they can recognise and interpret different approaches to assessment, and share expectations in areas such as coursework, orals and vivas, plagiarism and assessment regulations. Students used to cooperating very closely on practical assignments might find it difficult to recognise the boundaries between this and collaboration: this issue applies to students across the board, but can be most problematic when students have experienced diverse assessment expectations.

Similarly, students coming from countries with highly structured or even repressive regimes might have been accustomed to believing that there is one right way to perform a skill or to undertake an aesthetic practice, and might find the concept of originality of interpretation chal-lenging. For those coming from nations where dissent can be personally and physically dangerous, it is unsurprising if they adopt risk-averse strategies within aesthetic production.

Students might also need help in understanding what the marks they are given actually mean. The mark of C+ in some cultures is seen as an acceptable mid-point mark, whereas for a student from the US, for example, this would be regarded as a low grade. Pass marks vary hugely from context to context and nation to nation. In the UK a pass mark of 40 per cent is not uncommon, whereas a pass mark of 70 per cent is commonplace in the Netherlands. Students may be elated or disappointed inappropriately if they don't understand the system under which they are being assessed and they may interpret it as a sign of personal weakness or risking looking foolish if they ask for help. Time spent collectively helping students to unpack what criteria really mean, and on comments and feedback on assessed practice, is well-spent if it helps to produce shared understandings.

DESIGNING AN INCLUSIVE CURRICULUM

In designing taught programmes we should draw on international experience, thereby developing international perspectives within the classroom, and making the curriculum accessible for international students, as well as broadening perspectives for home students. In practice this means that when we design practical assignments we need to draw on curriculum content, examples and case studies that go beyond our own national boundaries in order to ensure that students from diverse backgrounds feel equally included. Cross-cultural sensitivity will need to be integrated into curriculum design, to ensure that students don't feel wrong-footed or discriminated against by the demands of an assignment. Managing the assessment of diverse students can be taxing for tutors who may be so concerned about doing or saying the wrong thing that their confidence is undermined. The main defence against this is to be open to guidance from well-informed colleagues and to be reflective about one's own personal practice, framing any mishaps as learning experiences. Many HEIs are today recognising as a staff development priority the need for cross-cultural awareness.

For those assessing students' artistic outputs, tutors need to be on their guard against privileging particular national perspectives on what comprises aesthetically pleasing results.

Marion Bowl, in her excellent study of diverse students going on to higher education from access courses in the West Midlands of the UK

(Bowl 2003), describes a mature Asian single parent studying on a pro-gramme where she learned about social disadvantage among unsupported families in Asian communities in Birmingham. Her tutor completely failed to draw out from the class any links between their own circum-stances or local knowledge and the material being studied, perhaps out of a sense of misplaced tact, with a result that the student concerned felt alienated and ignored. The experience impacted so powerfully on Bowl that she subtitled her book with a direct quote from the student: 'they talk about people like me' (Bowl 2003).

Some suggestions for ensuring equivalence of experience for diverse students when assessing practical skills:

- **Clarify what is expected in terms of originality.** In some cultures, including the ideas and even the precise original words of the teacher within assessed tasks is an expectation rather than something to be criticised, and a lack of shared understandings about this can lead to problems if not addressed early on. This can have particular repercussions in terms of accusations of plagiarism for practices that in other contexts are acceptable.
- **Be aware that assessment methods vary enormously from country to country.** What is common in one nation may be very unusual in others. In some places oral assessment is the norm, whereas elsewhere there is much more focus on time-constrained unseen exams. Students from some places will be happy and familiar with self- and peer assessment, while this might seem alien and odd to others.
- **Be inclusive in terms of cultural references in case study material.** Don't always use examples from the home nation, for example in business studies case studies, and avoid excessive references to cultural stereotypes, for example Asian family businesses. However, let students play to their own strengths in terms of selecting projects or tasks that relate to what they know about from their home contexts.
- **Similarly, avoid implying that all students are part of a particular age group when making cultural/social references that may marginalise older or younger students.** Students from an age group very different from your own are unlikely to have heard of many of the household names that are familiar to you.

- **Be cautious about assuming your own norms are universal.** For example, some students might find being asked to receive formative feedback on a live or practical task over a pint in the pub problematic, if their religious or social beliefs bar alcohol use.

- **Be aware of what a culture shock the HE environment can be for some students.** For example, some coming from very sheltered or secluded home and faith school environments might find the rough and tumble of student life quite frightening. An increase in home schooling by some black and minority ethnic families in the UK, for example, who are horrified by what they see as lax behavioural expectations from schools in the host community, means that some students are now entering HE without much experience of spending time in large, noisy and sometimes unruly classroom groups.

- **Remember that some students will be carrying huge familial expectations with them.** For these students, the prospect of failure will be particularly terrifying. Additionally, their families may not have a clear understanding of what student life in any particular country entails, which can lead to mismatched expectations. Rote-learning and wholesale recitation of substantial amounts of text is the norm in some religious groups, for example, so the concepts of experiential and independent learning particularly on practical courses may seem alien and inappropriate to some of our students' families, and hence to the students themselves if we do not brief and support them thoroughly and effectively.

- **Think about the language you use in giving feedback.** A term that you consider inoffensive might seem extremely rude to someone from a different culture, and the matey use of jargon or slang might be incomprehensible or confusing to someone who doesn't share your first language. Irony rarely translates well so is best avoided in oral feedback.

- **When assessing presentations, be aware that making eye contact with assessors of the opposite gender might be problematic.** Consider whether making eye contact really needs to be considered essential, and if it is, consider how much weighting is appropriate within the mark scheme.

- **Be sensitive about alternative arrangements for formal assessments that fall on religious festival dates.** This

45

should be considered at the outset rather than making last-minute arrangements. There may be implications, for example, if students are expected to undertake gruelling, lengthy assignments at times when they are likely to be fasting.

■ **Try to avoid making assumptions about the students you are assessing from the way they look.** We would all hope to avoid stereotyping by age, gender, apparel or stance, but it is not always easy to leave our own baggage behind when making judgements. Hence we should always aim to focus on the output or performance rather than the person.

Chapter 5

Fostering independent learning

Assessing self- and time-management skills

The development of independent learning skills has been a fundamental feature of higher education in the UK for many years. However, many students are now arriving in HE without the requisite practical study skills to be successful and often find themselves in trouble, not as a result of lack of aptitude in their academic subject but rather through their lack of abilities in project, time and self-management.

Although there is a growing body of web-based study skills resources available to students (see the bibliography and further reading for a list of sites that we recommend as student resources), the students most in need of support often lack the self-motivation or know-how to access these resources. Broader participation, improved opportunities for distance learning and ever-increasing external demands faced by many students require us to focus more than ever on the development and assessment of independent learning skills.

There is a range of simple techniques available for supporting the development of self-management and self-reflective skills. Jenny Moon (2004) suggests that learning journals containing ongoing reflection are useful for supporting planning, problem-solving and creative thinking activities, and in particular for 'uncovering areas of thinking that we would not normally come across'. She also suggests that concept maps or graphical displays may be useful, amongst other things, for supporting planning or as a means of exploring thinking processes.

Time management is the skill which above all others can make the difference between graduating and drop out.

Students go badly wrong when they:

- don't take charge of their own learning, harking back to the comfortable times when other people put pressure on them to keep on track;

- don't keep careful records of when work is due to be handed in, resulting in last-minute panics when they learn the news from their peers;
- are unable to organise their workloads sufficiently well in order to avoid missing deadlines;
- don't realise that handouts and printed materials are just information – they need to be worked with before they can count as learning;
- arrive late for, or are absent from, crucial briefing sessions at which detailed information about assignments is given out;
- don't catch up on what actually happened at teaching sessions they did not attend – even when their absence was unavoidable;
- start assignments at the last minute and then find they can't get hold of the resources they need to complete the task;
- believe it is a situation beyond their control if they are given multiple assignments with competing deadlines, rather than working out a plan whereby all can be achieved by starting early;
- have artificial expectations of how much they can achieve in any given period of time and then don't allow themselves sufficient time to complete tasks properly;
- are so determined to do a piece of work really well that they spend most of their energies on the research and thinking through stages, leaving insufficient time to bring it all together for the assignment;
- hand in coursework just hoping for the best, without first having self-assessed it against the given criteria, and improved it accordingly;
- ignore tutors' commentaries in live critiques and feedback on previous work, and don't make time to learn from it;
- regard critical feedback as failure, and stop trying, when they could have used the feedback as an opportunity to identify how best to develop their techniques;
- find plenty of displacement activities to avoid making a start on the really important task in hand;
- have too many other competing responsibilities going on in their lives to make it possible to allow enough time for coursework and production of artefacts;
- find themselves pressured by employers wanting them to work extra hours at crucial points when deadlines are looming, with a threat of being sacked if they don't comply;

■ don't read actively, failing to make notes in the text or on *Post-its* to help them find their way back to important data later.

Looking through this list are there any readers who don't recognise at least some of these behaviours in themselves? Substitute the words 'journal article' for 'assignment' and many of us will identify with quite a number of them in our own working lives.

However, to have become HE teachers/supporters of learning, we will all have had to develop our own coping strategies to enable us to leap these barriers in order to complete the many tasks that comprise the workload of an HE professional. It is these strategies we need to foster in our students if we are to help them become what Harding (2000: 77) calls 'incurable learners' that is, autonomous learners who have a range of transferable skills at their disposal that enable them to function effectively in a variety of contexts and at multiple levels.

 Case study 5.1

Lowri Blake of the Royal College of Music describes helping students to gain a better understanding of how learning happens both through teaching skills sessions in year 3 and through their own experiences of teaching others, something many music students do to supplement their income while at college (Hunter 2004: 91). She quotes a fourth year piano undergraduate student as saying, 'I'm learning so much about my own practice and playing, now that I've started teaching'. They also develop self-awareness through the use of personal development plans, which are 'seen as an important element in the process of development as a musician, helping the student to become more confident, independent and self-directed as a learner'.

Students sometimes believe that effective time management is a characteristic rather than behaviour, that is, something that you inherently have or have not, rather than a pattern of activity that can be learned. It is not usually sufficient, therefore, to show students what good time management looks like and expect them to emulate it: for this reason activities based around time management sometimes form part of an assessed activity in programmes aiming to foster effective learning.

Case study 5.2

Students studying on the second year of the BA Hons in Business Information Systems at Sheffield Hallam University can take an elective module which allows them to develop soft systems methodology skills. Assessment is via a full soft systems analysis of a fictitious student accommodation letting agency. Students work in teams on a six-week project identifying problems with the business. Teams are responsible not only for project and time management (meeting with tutors for weekly progress checks), but also for identifying and addressing their learning needs. During the project, for example, they have the opportunity to interview members of staff role-playing the two very different partners of the agency in order to elicit the views of the partners, request agency documentation or seek clarification on any other areas of the problem situation.

(Heather Clothier, Sheffield Hallam University)

Some disabilities may make a student more likely to find time management and self-organisation difficult, including some forms of dyslexia. It is difficult to balance a desire to treat students as independent and autonomous learners with the need to provide appropriate support to help them become so over time (Adams and Brown 2006). For this reason, a 'scaffolding' approach is often adopted. In practice this means that significant support is provided in the early stages, which is progressively withdrawn as students become better able to manage their own learning. This needs to be done sensitively, with the approach being made explicit, so that students don't feel abandoned once they are left to their own devices.

In the transition into HE, Bowl (2003), among others, has identified the negative effect of sudden change in levels of support that mature students coming from access programmes sometimes experience when moving from a highly structured and very supportive learning environment into higher education, where they feel they are left to sink or swim on their own.

Bowl describes the shock students experience on entering higher education:

There are ways in which teacher habitus on the one hand, and the new environment of higher education on the other, work together to distance students from their teachers and tutors and to downgrade the pedagogic and supportive aspects of university learning. The onus is on the student to learn, to find her own way, or to give up the course. Once in higher education the students in this study faced difficulty in adjusting to its rules and norms, which were often tacit rather than explicit. Adjustment involved learning to write in a style and language appropriate to higher education. It was not simply a matter of spelling and grammar, but involved learning to subjugate their own substantial life experience to the experience of the academy. For students who had arrived at university by non A-level routes, this was sometimes difficult. Access courses, particularly those in the social sciences, had stressed the value of using their personal experience as material for discussion. Higher education did not.

(Bowl 2003: 143–4)

She further commented on the ways in which they saw their struggles as a matter of personal responsibility, and indeed shame:

In trying to make the shift from using their own style of expression, participants sometimes seemed to overcompensate by lifting large chunks of writing from books, rather than reading, paraphrasing and referencing authors' work, and ultimately becoming confused about what it was that their tutors required. The students were unwilling to seek clarification of confusing assignment tasks and blamed themselves for their failure to understand what was required of them. As relative novices, they found reading academic language difficult. They saw failure to understand as their own failure rather than as a failure to communicate on the part of writers and academics. In doing so, they contributed to their own sense of exclusion from the world of high status learning. Once again, self blame is a powerful force in perpetuating a sense of exclusion.

(Bowl 2003: 134)

For this reason, HEIs with high numbers of non-traditional students are increasingly exploring intensive transition programmes for first year students entering HE for the first time. For example, in one faculty at Leeds Metropolitan University the first three weeks are taught as a foundation project with students receiving significant amounts of additional guidance about effective learning behaviours, and then throughout the remainder of the first year teaching and assessment are structured in six-week blocks to support regular feedback.

51

Case study 5.3

The authors have used the tongue-in-cheek guidance below as part of the induction process, in a role-playing exercise where 'Bruce' (recumbent, can of lager in hand) offers students a guide to having a really good time at university. This is designed to get them thinking about their own time and self-management skills. This was followed by a plenary (out of role) in which these kinds of behaviour were linked to research literature on student performance and attrition. A linked task could invite students to identify the behaviours that align most closely with their own bad practices and to write a short reflection on how they can combat their own backsliding ways.

The drongo's guide to studying in higher education

Forget about induction. You just have to listen to a lot of boring stuff of no earthly use so you might as well use the time more productively getting to know the locality (and the locals).

Don't bother going on the library/resource centre familiarisation tour. You won't learn anything useful. All libraries are much the same, just loads of old, mouldering books written by deadbeats of no earthly use to students studying modern subjects. Anyway, if you want a book you can just go in and ask the librarian to find it for you.

You've got better things to spend your money on than books. After all, if it's really important, they'll have what you need in the library won't they?

Look after any set texts you get hold of really well, and then you can get your money back on them from university bookshops when you leave. Whatever you do, don't write any notes in the margin of your books or mark them in any way – that will make them hard to sell on.

If you get ill or have problems, keep it to yourself. University is for adults not kids, and it's none of their business if you're having a bad time. There's nothing they can do to help anyway, is there?

If your tutor asks you to go and see him or her, only go along if there's something you want to ask. For the most part they are not really interested in students and just want to get on with their research. Bothering them with your trivia will just get their backs up.

You'll need a part-time job to keep you in funds. Don't worry, it doesn't matter how many hours you work, you can still fit your study in alongside your work. And don't forget that working unsocial hours (all-night café, night club) often pays best.

Don't bother to use a diary. Only wimps do that. You were bright enough to get into university so you should be clever enough to keep all the deadlines for assignment submissions and other dates in your head.

Pencil cases belong back in primary school. You're bound to be able to scrounge a pen and some paper from someone else. Anyway, with these fees we're paying, shouldn't the tutor provide them?

If they give you lots of assignments with the same handing-in date, they can't expect you to do them all well, so do what you can. If they can't be bothered to organise things sensibly, why should you do other than the minimum in order to just get something handed in?

Don't waste your money on materials for practical projects. Your university should be supplying all the resources you need, shouldn't they? You've got better things to spend your money on.

If you get a bad mark, don't read all those comments your tutor writes on your work. It will only depress you. Chuck the assignment in the back of your cupboard and move swiftly on. There's no point going over the old stuff.

If you get towards the end of the semester and you've got loads of course work, stop going to all the remaining teaching sessions. There's only so much you can take in at any one time and it's hardly likely they'll be doing crucial stuff right at the end, is it?

If you have to work in a group, don't give too much away to the others. They just want to steal your best ideas and take the credit. If you just go along to the sessions and let others do all the work, you'll come out fine without pushing yourself too hard.

Actually, group work is a waste of time, so don't go along to the sessions at all. You'll only learn anything useful from the tutors, anyway.

Your most important information source on your course is your mates. Why bother looking at notice boards or on the web if someone else will do it for you?

Nine o'clock lectures are for losers. No one cool goes in for the early starts, and anyway you can get everything you need from one of the terminally sad people who did get out of bed in time.

53

No one bothers with Friday afternoon sessions. If the university felt it was something important, they wouldn't timetable it for a time when most people don't plan to turn up.

In fact, why bother going in at all? There are plenty of examples of people who never go into classes and work on their own at home and who still manage to pass all the assignments.

Party, party, party. Get your priorities right! You're only young once and no one loves a party-pooper.

The best night for getting blasted is Sunday. It gets you off to a really good start to the week if you have a few drinks with your mates before the drudgery sets in.

All the rumours linking drug use and depression/dropping out are just scare-mongering. Why not get out of your head every day: it's what student life is for!

Save a tree: don't pick up handouts. They only go over the same stuff you hear in lectures, so you're hardly likely to pick up anything new.

Only obsessive deviants have a filing system. Of course you'll remember where you've put your lecture notes. Anyway, the assessments are only at the end of the semester so you're hardly likely to misplace things in that short time.

There's no need to do any work until just before the deadline. It's no fun slogging away all the time and in any case all the papers say university life is a doddle nowadays.

You're at a reputable university, so you can trust the printers to work reliably. This means you can gain extra time by working right up to the last minute then popping in to use the printer just before the deadline. No worries!

No need to back up your work. IT systems are really reliable nowadays and in any case your tutor will be sympathetic if you lose the final draft.

If things start going badly wrong with your course, you might as well throw in the towel. None of the staff will be prepared to help you get yourself out of a jam. You're only a number to them anyway.

FOSTERING INDEPENDENT LEARNING IN OTHER VULNERABLE GROUPS

Whilst students new to HE are perhaps particularly vulnerable to falling into poor study habits, there are other groups of students for which the development of independent learning skills is very important. Targeted diagnostic assessment of learning skills prior to commencement of distance learning can help students who have never used this type of learning previously to understand its specialist requirements. Most would expect postgraduates, who by definition have been effective at study previously, to have a battery of skills at their disposal, but this is sadly not always the case. Furthermore, there are likely to be advanced skills they will need to use to help them be effective in novel contexts and with potentially less direction than they would have been used to at undergraduate level (Farrar 2006).

 Case study 5.4

Foundation Direct, one of the University of Portsmouth's centres for excellence in teaching and learning (CETL), is developing a 'home-grown' variant of the e-portfolio for the university's foundation degrees in the form of a succession of progress reports that are the assessed elements of personal development planning (PDP) units offered at levels 1 and 2. Mid-unit and end of unit (or end of foundation degree) reports count toward assessment. The professional development units also deliver online structured learning support and generic professional development learning activities in a blended learning mode.

For the units, students are required to record the whole learning from the PDP unit and elsewhere on the degree in the three domains: academic or subject knowledge, practice knowledge and personal knowledge (values, career aspirations, etc.). As the students progress, the area of overlap between the three domains is expected to grow.

Students are supported in writing progress reports from the start of their courses when they commence with an on-entry formative assessment or 'benchmark statement', against which progress noted in later reports is to be measured. Students will be drawn into measuring their progress using profession-specific standards. Support is provided in the form of online exercises, threaded online discussions and exemplar progress reports.

55

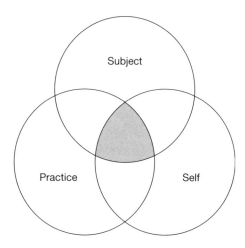

FIGURE 5.1 Overlap between the three domains

Progress reports are appraised by mentors and their comments added before being forwarded to the university or college tutor for marking on a 'good pass', 'pass', 'fail' basis, using criteria that cover:

■ planning and managing learning and work;
■ reflection on learning;
■ the quality of the written report.

A good pass would be indicated by a student who:

■ reflects on his/her work management;
■ contributes to the online discussion board;
■ sets own career targets and post-foundation degree learning goals;
■ reports on developed approaches to work and study;
■ critically reviews own practice in relation to the senior practitioner skills areas and associated theory and principles;
■ critically reviews development or changes to own values about Early Years education;
■ cites examples of researching, evaluating and the use of theory to develop practice in their own place of work.

(Frank Lyons, Foundation Degree PDP, University of Portsmouth)

Some tips on assessing students' independent learning skills:

- **Investigate a range of ways in which students can demonstrate effective independent learning skills.** These are likely to include learning logs, PDPs, reflective commentaries, e-portfolios and other forms of assessment based on self-reflection.

- **Consider offering incentives other than summative assessment for participating in recording and reflecting on independent learning skills.** This may or may not include marks, but feedback is essential. Other incentives might include prize draws for those submitting learning logs.

- **Use the assessment process to clarify what you want the students to achieve and which skills they will need.** Ensure that students have a clear understanding of what is required of them. Make the criteria and weightings reflect the activities and approaches you want to privilege.

- **Consider using models of good practice to enable students to self-assess the first activities.** Models can be really helpful to students having difficulty in understanding exactly what you want them to do. Having got the hang of the process, they are then likely to be able to continue independently.

- **Ask students to submit a self-assessment sheet when submitting work.** Brown (Brown *et al.* 1994) and Race (2001) both suggest that this can be useful to both student and tutor in identifying areas and strategies for improvement.

- **Try out self-assessment worksheets to assess time management skills.** Activities of this type encourage students to take a close look at how they are spending their time and support class discussion and peer support.

- **Consider setting an early task inviting students to design a job description for an effective student.** As well as being an assessed task, the outputs are likely to be usable in tutorials or group discussions as a basis for developing shared understandings.

- **Think about introducing students to project-based and problem-based learning.** For the development of independent learning it is helpful to focus on the process rather than the product of learning.

57

- **Keep students busy.** If we are hoping to support the development of project and time management skills this is best achieved by giving students challenges, and opportunities to develop coping strategies.
- **Consider rationing student–tutor contact time at higher levels.** Students are more likely to value meetings and tutorials if they are regarded as a limited resource for which they need to plan.
- **Recognise the particular needs of postgraduate students.** Postgraduate students can feel isolated and lost when faced with a significant project with long timescales and little peer interaction.
- **Consider the use of online self-assessment quizzes.** Many students find these interesting and unthreatening to complete, and can identify their own areas for development or recognise where their skills lie.
- **Recognise the importance of developing and supporting the time management skills of students taking distance learning courses.** Be cautious in using distance learning assessment for students who have not evidenced independent learning skills.
- **Don't assume that your students, however mature and experienced, have no need of further coaching on effective study techniques.** Even old hands can gain from fresh approaches and alternative techniques to manage their learning.

Chapter 6

Assessing presentations and other oral work

> When I was peer observed delivering a large lecture I felt like someone was grading my kissing. All pleasure was removed as I concentrated on my technique and it definitely resulted in a lesser performance.
>
> (Deb, 39, experienced lecturer)

> We normally have show and tell on a Friday. We've done it ever since reception. It's really boring. When Nicola had her ears pierced she brought these earrings in five times. Laura loves being the centre of attention and always gets up first and talks for ages. She always brings in photos of her puppy. At first I was a bit jealous but then she brought it in for pets' day and it pooed all over the playground.
>
> (Sheila, aged 9)

TO ASSESS OR NOT TO ASSESS?

It is arguable in some quarters whether the assessment of presentation skills has a place in higher education; whether a student's ability to orally present is any more worthy of explicit assessment at this level than other basic communication skills such as the ability to spell. Yet the general acceptance that an ability to make a presentation is a desirable graduate attribute has been used to justify the assessment of presentation skills on many HE courses over recent years.

There exists, however, a paradox. If we accept that the best presentations are so engaging that we do not consciously register the presenter's skills, then how can we validly assess these transparent skills? If we are to do this in a higher education context, we need to approach the matter very systematically.

By focusing on oral presentation skills and by explicitly assessing these skills separately from the content of a presentation, we may well reduce the likelihood that students will come to regard oral presentations as a natural form of communication and hence exploit the medium appropriately, in that the act of assessing presentation skills may affect that presentation and subsequent presentations detrimentally. We need to establish exactly why we are assessing oral skills and what it is that we are attempting to assess. This will vary between courses, disciplines and levels.

Whilst the necessity to assess the advocacy skills of a final year student on a law course is incontrovertible, the rationale for including a formal 30-minute presentation in the first semester of a computing degree is less clear.

Equally, where it is the case that students are being asked to prepare and deliver a large number of presentations on a course, the justification needs to be considered carefully, particularly where the same skills are being assessed several times.

Many students find presentations intimidating and may be disadvantaged by an over-reliance on this type of assessment. It is therefore important that tutors consider the range of alternative oral assessment formats available and select the most appropriate format for the assessment.

At Alverno College in the US the teaching, development and assessment of presentation skills is integral to all courses at all levels, with the expectation that student achievement will improve and therefore be assessed at higher levels at different stages within a programme. This makes much more sense than many systems where presentations are included in many modules within a programme, with no coherent approach to track improvement or added value over time. As a very minimum, we should expect to see the criteria on which students are being judged becoming more sophisticated from level one to level three of a programme.

THE MODERN CONTEXT: ORAL COMMUNICATION REQUIREMENTS

Historically the most effective and therefore most valued vehicles of oral communication – the pulpit, the lectern, radio, TV and video – have all required of their exponents oratory and presentation skills.

However, we need to recognise that there has been a significant change in the communication methods employed on a daily basis in virtually every area of society. We have moved rapidly to a world characterised by synchronous, rich, interactive, on-demand, two-way communication.

Whilst the possession of oral skills is, in a world characterised by such a vast array of communications opportunities, more important than ever, an ability to deliver a formal presentation is relatively far less important than it was, having being superseded by the requirement for clear, concise, continual interaction.

As more and more oral communication is at a distance, supported via the Internet, mobile communications technologies, video conferencing and multimedia presentations, it is important that we do not restrict our assessment of students' oral skills to formal one-way face-to-face presentations.

The student's oral experience can be enriched by a variety of assessment formats. More interactive formats such as vivas, seminars, showcases and debates, in addition to preparing students for employability, allow tutors to probe and can consequently be more efficient in establishing both student learning and communication skills than a traditional presentation. It's therefore important that the tutor consider where alternative and more innovative assessment of oral skills may be appropriate.

THE PROBLEM WITH PRESENTATIONS

The availability and ease of producing an automated PowerPoint presentation has seen a trend towards reading aloud to an audience in a way that encourages fatigue and boredom. This over-reliance on visual aids and technology is a modern phenomenon not restricted to education ('death by PowerPoint').

Care should be taken in the design of assessment criteria to discourage presentations of this format and to encourage responsiveness to audience and spontaneity.

Another major issue in the assessment of oral presentations is the tutor time required for assessment. Where it is considered desirable for students to present orally, tutors should consider how it may be practicable to reduce the burden of assessment on staff. Team presentations, for example, can have benefits for both students and tutors. It is also worth considering limiting presentation times. A five-minute presentation focusing on key points can be more demanding of students than a 30-minute ramble, and reduces the likelihood of tutor fatigue and the possible consequential reduction in reliability of assessment.

WHAT ARE WE ASSESSING?

The most important critical success factor in the assessment of oral and presentation skills is the specification and communication of clear assessment criteria. First, we should decide the relative weighting of content and delivery. Second, we should identify the intended outcome of the presentation – is it to communicate findings? To persuade an audience? To inspire? We should also consider whether to explicitly identify marks for creativity and originality.

From the detailed assessment criteria we should be able to:

- select the most appropriate form of assessment. For example, assessing an individual's speeches within a debate would perhaps be most appropriate where the ability to persuade an audience is an intended outcome. A group presentation may be best when teamwork is a priority, while a moot might be the ideal means of assessing students' advocacy skills on a law degree;
- judge whether it would be appropriate to involve others, including fellow students, clients, end-users, invited guests or the general public in the assessment.

SELF-ASSESSMENT

The general availability of video equipment in many universities enables students to video their own and each other's presentations. These may then be studied for formative self-assessment prior to summative assessment by others. This could be formalised by a student presenting their reflections.

Often significant development can be achieved by students reviewing their own presentations on video using semi-structured prompts to aid reflection. This might include initially asking students merely to describe what they see on video, aiming to avoid excessive self-criticism too early on, then moving towards being more analytic and critiquing their performance with a view to improving it, perhaps using peers to offer reality checks. Processes such as inter-personal recall techniques can be used to formalise this, so that the formative review can be a positive rather than a negative experience (who other than rock stars and small children can watch themselves on video without cringing?).

AUDIENCE ASSESSMENT

Different aspects of a presentation may be assessed by a number of people consecutively. Subject tutors and external experts could assess content whilst communications specialists assess the presentation skills and students from lower years assess comprehensibility and usefulness. Consideration should be given to making the assessment of a presentation as efficient as possible and where possible to *use* the presentation for an authentic purpose.

PEER ASSESSMENT

Presentations are potentially an excellent means of introducing peer assessment, as evaluation by the audience will give the presenter feedback and makes the experience less boring for the audience who otherwise would be passive. It may also offer a good formative learning experience to peer assessors who can thereby improve their own presentation skills as a result.

Indeed it should be considered whether some part of a student's marks should be given for their assessment of others' presentations. This could take the form of a reflective critical evaluation by the assessing students which is then reviewed by the tutor.

For peer assessment to be successful we must specify clearly which aspects of the presentation we are expecting the audience to assess. Negotiation of the criteria to be used by peers assessing one another's presentations can be a really useful way of helping students to get inside the criteria and to understand how what they are doing matches up to required standards. It can be useful to provide a video of a presentation containing a lot of errors (one prepared in advance by the tutor, hamming it up outrageously, can provide excellent entertainment value while providing useful discussion points).

Proformas are useful in directing assessors and also save tutor time in post-presentation moderation.

If a student audience is required to give immediate feedback to a presenter, then issues relating to a lack of anonymity may reasonably be expected to affect that feedback, which may be a disadvantage in terms of frankness and sensitivity.

Personal response systems ('zappers') and other electronic systems now used in many institutions potentially offer a solution to this problem, feedback being anonymous to the presenter but auditable by the tutor (to guard against bias). Feedback via mobile phone and texts can offer similar advantages because it can provide immediate feedback.

Of course, if presentations are delivered online then anonymous peer assessment moderated by the tutor is far simpler to achieve. The technology available in many universities today offers opportunities for peers to formatively feed back on each other's work. Videoed student presentations can, for example, be posted on the intranet for feedback either in place of or prior to a final face-to-face presentation.

TEAM PRESENTATIONS

Where teams of students are required to design and deliver a collaborative presentation there are many advantages in terms of assessment. First, of course, there are fewer assessments to mark and moderate. Second, if students are to be marked as a team, they have a vested interest in improving others' performances. Team members can therefore be expected to formatively assess each other's presentation skills. This could take place without the tutor being present, prior to the summative assessment.

Where students are involved in assessing presentations by other groups, either formatively or summatively, they will need careful briefing and rehearsal to foster shared understandings of what comprises good and less effective presentations and to encourage a focus on the achievements rather than the personalities of the presenters. As with many other forms of assessment, students will need encouragement to ensure they are constantly striving to match evidence of achievement against the agreed criteria. It is sometimes possible for students (and indeed tutors!) to be seduced by showy and entertaining presentations that are shallow or contain incorrect material, and similarly for markers to downgrade worthy but dull presentations, especially when suffering from assessment fatigue.

Viva voce ('live voice') exams are most commonly used in the UK for assessing postgraduate research but are more widely used in countries including the Netherlands and Sweden both as an anti-plagiarism device and because they are useful in providing opportunities to probe learning in greater detail than can be the case when written assignments are set.

Assessed seminars, where students take turns over a number of weeks to prepare material that they then present to fellow students in the tutor's presence, can be a valuable means of encouraging and checking independent learning. Involving students in assessing others' presentations can be helpful to ensure that their attention remains focused and can be a useful learning experience for them in its own right. Of course, care must be taken in these cases immediately to correct any misinformation contained within students' presentations to one another and to clarify any ambiguities in subsequent discussions, ideally without resorting to completely taking over the seminar.

Case study 6.1

A tutor was concerned that his students were only engaging seriously in assessed presentations when it was their turn to present. He encouraged higher levels of involvement by issuing cards at the beginning of each seminar on which students in the audience were encouraged to make notes from their peers' presentations. These cards were handed in at the end of each seminar and one mark per session was credited to the students' total (maximum ten marks for ten attendances). These cards were then returned to students in the ensuing exam as 'aides memoires' to the material discussed. As a result of this endeavour attendance at and involvement in peers' seminars increased and some improvement was noted in exam performance across the cohort.

Some tips on assessing presentations and other oral work:

- **Make explicit the purpose and assessment criteria of student presentation.** Ensure that students are clear about the weighting of criteria for consideration, for example of accuracy of content, fluency and use of audio-visual aids. Is the focus of this presentation primarily on knowledge demonstrated, or on the ability to put it across well?
- **Use the audience to contribute to the assessment process.** Not only will you engage the non-presenting students in purposeful activity that will make it less likely that they will be disruptive, but the experience of assessing presentations is likely to be valuable to them.
- **Record or video presentations to allow self-assessment and reflection.** You will need to find ways to set this up so as to be as unobtrusive as possible, and to accept that some

65

students will find being recorded rather off-putting the first time they experience it. However, the benefits of having a means of recording what would otherwise be an ephemeral experience and to use it for subsequent self- and peer critique are likely to far outweigh any disadvantages.

- **Use team presentations on occasion.** One basic advantage is that they can cut down the total number of presentations that have to be reviewed and assessed. Another is that, set up appropriately, they can be used to foster and demonstrate collective learning. However, it is important to establish early on that you don't just want groups to divide tasks in the presentation so that what you actually watch is a number of micro-presentations, with no attempt to make it a cohesive group effort.

- **Consider varied methods of assessing orally including showcasing, critiques and vivas.** Each will have benefits and disadvantages, but by using a range of approaches you will enable diverse students to demonstrate their talents to the full.

- **Keep presentations quite short.** Students should be encouraged to recognise that part of the skill of making an impact orally is to be succinct. Brevity will also be appreciated by students for whom the whole business is an ordeal, and by tutors with large groups to avoid the process running on into several days.

- **Consider involving and/or inviting sponsors and clients in assessment.** Bringing in external experts not only spreads the load of assessment, but also offers the potential for authentic assessments by those who know the context best. Of prime importance, however, is the need to ensure inter-assessor consistency.

- **Consider banning the use of notes and restricting visual aids.** This is likely to be particularly valuable once students have done some initial assessed presentations and are likely to have the confidence to work without too many props.

- **Encourage students to engage in formative practice in front of each other when the tutor is not present.** This is likely to help them develop expertise, but be aware that unmediated critique by peers may be significantly more robust than that they allow tutors to see and hear!

- **Use a single presentation to assess synoptically.**
  Learning from several parts of the course can be brought
  together in a single assessed presentation, both encouraging
  students to make links between disparate areas of the course
  and making the assessment process potentially more efficient.
- **Use vivas productively.** Give students the opportunity to
  role play vivas in advance of the real thing, with students taking
  it in turn to ask questions on a topic, answer questions and act
  as an observer. The process of formulating suitable questions
  and feeding back both on the questioning and the responding
  will give students insights into the viva process.
- **Consider how best to ensure full participation in
  assessed seminars.** Clarity concerning criteria and evidence
  of achievement against them is essential from the outset,
  whether these provided by the tutor or negotiated by the
  group.
- **Ensure that organisation of the assessment process is
  undertaken in good time.** You don't want to add to
  students' (or your own) stress levels by being disorganised
  about timing, feedback sheets or process.
- **Consider offering immediate oral feedback.** Students,
  particularly those for whom oral presentations are unfamiliar
  or very trying, will appreciate being given some indication
  relatively early as to how they have done, rather than stewing
  over every perceived failing in their performance.
- **Consider allowing the submission of a team-produced
  video of their team presentation.** This will have the
  advantage of letting them cut and edit the video footage until
  they are happy with the outcome, which is likely to be
  appreciated by students who for personal or cultural reasons
  find live oral presentations difficult. It could also rule out some
  of the organisational problems experienced by tutors in terms
  of room bookings and timing and would allow the tutor to pace
  the assessment process, rather than sitting through what may
  feel like endless and perhaps repetitive presentations.
- **Explore ways of recoding evidence of oral assessment.**
  As well as the more obvious means (including audio and
  video tape), you could also consider using a dictaphone
  yourself to comment on what you see and hear. Alternatively,
  or additionally, you could ask students to submit a short,

67

reflective commentary on their performance and the feedback they received for audit and moderation purposes.

- **Allow students opportunities for rehearsal prior to the assessment.** This will enable less confident students to get the measure, for example, of the room in which they will be presenting and can also help them to get a feel for timing, check out audio-visual facilities and generally troubleshoot the process.

- **Aim to ensure inclusivity with oral assessment.** Be aware that some disabled students will need to be offered alternative assignments (but always check with the student concerned before putting these in place, as the student him/herself is likely to be best placed to advise on what is and what is not possible). Similarly, check with students whose religious or cultural beliefs you suspect might make oral assessments problematic and offer equivalent assignments as appropriate.

- **Keep referring back to the learning outcomes that are being assessed by this particular assignment.** Check, for example, whether the prime focus is on material learned for which this is the demonstration, or whether it is mainly an assessment of a group process.

- **Remember that the challenge of an oral assessment will be different for various students, depending on their previous life experiences.** For those who have been doing presentations throughout their sixth form, they will hold no fears. For others, who perhaps have been out of education for many years or who come from a country where oral assessments are very unfamiliar, this may well be terrifyingly alien!

Chapter 7

Assessing practical skills in laboratories

Laboratory work has always been a feature of science, health, environmental and engineering subjects, and each of these subjects has evolved specialist approaches to the assessment of laboratory-based practical skills.

A particular feature of education at all levels in the last couple of decades has been the rise of another kind of laboratory – the computer lab. Although at some times these computer labs are used as free access student resources, at other times they are used to assess the practical computing skills students develop in these labs, or for computer-assisted assessment (CAA) to assess practical (and other) skills.

This chapter describes and evaluates traditional and emerging methods used to assess practical skills in a range of laboratories. We will discuss ways in which lab-based assessment can be designed and implemented to ensure efficient use of both student and staff time, and consider methods to guard against inappropriate or even fraudulent practice in labs. The growing use of CAA and other technologies to support assessment of practical skills in labs is also considered.

PROBLEMS WITH ASSESSING PRACTICAL SKILLS IN LABS

There are a number of issues relating to the assessment of laboratory skills. It is often the case that where laboratory experience is part of a course, this is not actually assessed but viewed as a valuable experience for students to support and underpin their wider course studies. However, as students become increasingly strategic in their approach to their studies, and increasingly assessment driven, this may result in less value being given to the development of practical skills that are not assessed.

Traditionally:

- Many departments have staffed laboratories with research assistants and senior students rather than with experienced lecturers.
- Where laboratory skills have been assessed this has tended to be based on the outcome, result or the product of the enquiry.

There is clearly potential for overlooking flaws in the practical process and it can be difficult to isolate, if there is a problem, where that problem might be. There may also be issues relating to plagiarism of results between students of the same cohort, the passing of results from the previous cohort to the next and, of course, trading in results over the Internet.

The necessity to design more reliable assessment of laboratory skills comes at a time when many science departments are reducing their laboratory expenditure and looking for ways to make assessment more efficient and cost-effective. The assessment of some key skills, for example the ability to carry out experiments accurately and safely, present particular challenges if the option of time-consuming and expensive observation is not available. So which methods are best suited to the assessment of laboratory skills?

LABORATORY WRITE-UP REPORTS

Lab write-ups are still the most commonly used method of assessment of practical skills in many laboratories, and they can be useful in assessing knowledge of experimental procedures, analysis and interpretation of results. Typically a lab write-up report comprises of introduction, methods, results, processing, interpretation, discussion of outcomes and reasons for deviations from the expected results. Sometimes written questions are set to test understanding. These lab write-ups are then marked and returned to students with feedback prior to the next laboratory session.

The lab write-up is often over-used, and a major weakness of the method is that it does not measure practical skills but rather *knowledge* of practical skills. This method of assessment relies very much on students recording and manipulating results. Accuracy and errors may only be assessed by looking at these results.

TABLE 7.1 Assessing lab write-ups

Strategy for assessment of lab write-ups	Advantages over traditional write-up	Issues with approach
Students work in teams. Team (rather than individual) report is submitted.	Opportunities for peer teaching and improved learning. Reduces marking load.	Does not address the problem of students under-utilising the tutor's feedback.
Mark only a sample or selection of the laboratory exercises.	Reduces marking load.	If students are aware which write-ups will not be marked there may be reduced effort. Does not address student under-utilisation of feedback.
Marking carried out by postgraduate students rather than tutors.	Reduces academic staff's marking load.	May be inconsistency of marking. Does not address student under-utilisation of feedback.
Ask students to submit their write-ups using a workbook, grid or some other specified format.	Reduces marking time.	Removes student initiative. Completed workbooks can easily be passed from cohort to cohort.
Use MCQs to test understanding of the practical.	Can be computer assessed removing marking load completely. Immediate feedback can be provided.	Report writing skills are not developed.
Peer assess write-ups.	Reduces staff marking load significantly.	Requires clear and explicit marking guidelines. May improve the standard of subsequent practical write-ups.

A reliance on this method of assessment can also result in difficulties in assessing the higher order cognitive skills, and in high student and staff workload.

However, given that on many programmes the lab write-up remains the predominant mode of assessment of laboratory skills, a number of modified lab write-up approaches can be taken. Ian Hughes identified two major problems with the traditional use of lab write-ups in the biosciences, which can be generalised to other subjects:

1   Significant amounts of staff time are required to mark them, particularly when student groups and/or the number of lab sessions are large.
2   Feedback written on the laboratory write-up by staff is often not read by students, who are often only concerned with the mark awarded.

A variety of strategies which can be adopted to address these issues are outlined in Table 7.1 (adapted from Hughes 2004).

Each of these approaches may, in the right circumstances, be effective in reducing the significant burden of lab write-up assessment. More significantly, a number of these approaches, particularly group working, the use of computer assisted assessment and peer marking provide opportunities for formative feedback and improved student learning. However, most of these strategies are based on an assumption that lab work will be assessed via lab reports. Alternative forms of assessment for lab work may offer possible benefits and outcomes.

 Case study 7.1

Dave Rodgers, in the School of Built Environment at Leeds Metropolitan University, asks large groups of engineering surveyor students to prepare maps and plans for the planning and design of structures, and ensures that the construction takes place to the dimensions and tolerances specified in the design. Students have to be assessed in their ability both to use the equipment and to manipulate/analyse the observed data. Formative assessment using the e-learning environment is utilised to simultaneously reduce the marking load and improve student feedback.

The first formative assessment can be started at the end of week two and must be submitted by the end of week five. Each formative practical assessment has an electronic booking sheet that students download over WebCT. The practical work is done in groups of four or five, but the computational work is done on an individual basis. Each student is assigned a unique numerical value that makes the computations specific to them. The observations and unique numerical value are entered into the electronic booking sheet, along with the results of their calculations. Error messages will be displayed if there are any obvious errors in the data input. The results are then submitted electronically over WebCT.

When the submission date has passed, the lecturer downloads the electronic submissions and visually checks each one to ensure that the student has met the coursework requirements. At this stage, a password is made available to the students over WebCT; this is used to unlock hidden workbooks that contain pre-written formulae that take the students' observed data and unique numerical value and then compute and display a complete set of computations and answers that are specific to the individual student, who can then compare his/her version of the computations with the correct version. If they do not agree with the calculations and cannot find the error, they are required to seek out the tutor for further explanation.

Before introducing this approach, it was difficult to determine if the students' work was their own, especially when the observational data was inevitably the same for groups of students and staff workload was high. Marking and correcting scripts was formerly taking long hours, with no guarantee that students would read the scribbled corrections/comments, especially when the work was not returned to them for considerable periods. In the new system, each student is able to get a print-out of the correct calculations based on his/her own specific data the day after the closing date for submissions. This method of assessment has generally been very successful. Any problems experienced are largely concerned with access to IT systems, for example by off-site part-time students. To get round this problem, copies of the downloadable booking sheets are made available to part-time students on disc or CD.

OBJECTIVE STRUCTURED CLINICAL EXAMINATIONS

The objective structured clinical examination (OSCE) is a form of assessment initially used in medicine to assess clinical competence and practical skills.

Typically students rotate through a series of stations where they are asked to perform procedures. Assessment is via experts at each station. Although quite complex and time-consuming to design and organise, this mode of assessment is easy to score and provide feedback on. There may be the potential to involve other students as 'patients' or 'clients' at each station, which can be useful formative activity for both examinee and subject. The OSCE is best exploited as an assessment method where feedback is given immediately at each station. It may also lend itself to peer assessment activity. OSCEs can be used in induction programmes to assess key practical skills, and later in programmes to test performance against outcomes and provide feedback. Group OSCEs can be particularly useful for teaching and feedback. Although several assessors are required at one time, OSCEs are probably less labour intensive than other forms of marking. Although the use of OSCEs has spread through a whole range of subject areas from business to social work as a useful way to quickly assess practical skills, their potential for the assessment of laboratory skills has perhaps not been fully exploited.

 Case study 7.2

OSCEs are widely used in medicine and related professions, but have been adapted for other contexts, for example for the police, where they are known as Objective Structured Practical Examinations (OSPREYs). Boursicot and Roberts (2005) describe an OSCE as 'an assessment format in which the candidates rotate around a circuit of stations, at each of which specific tasks have to be performed, usually involving clinical skills such as history taking or examination of a patient'. They advise that:

- ■ OSCEs are not suitable for all aspects of clinical knowledge.
- ■ It is important to determine the context at the outset and map this against the learning outcomes.
- ■ Feasibility of tasks must be carefully checked, for example use of live or simulated patients (SPs).
- ■ 'Station material' needs to be written well in advance of the assessment date, including instructions for student and examiners, equipment requirements, requirements for real patients or SPs, patient scenarios (if used) prepared, duration of tasks and marking schedules.
- ■ Prior to the OSCE, suitable venues will have to be chosen, appropriate examiners recruited and timetabled, any SPs recruited, stations will need to be numbered, equipment listed, mark sheets prepared (possibly allowing for electronic scanning) and clinical skills centre staff briefed.
- ■ On the day of the OSCE, room signage will need to be put up, timing indicators (electronic or manually operated loud bells) organised, helpers/marshals recruited and briefed to ensure smooth running, catering arrangements made for refreshment breaks, and candidates briefed.
- ■ After the OSCE, mark sheets will need to be collected, patients/SPs transported home and/or paid (as appropriate) and thank you letters sent.

- Any SPs should be well trained and chosen for representative diversity, with scenarios provided in advance and rehearsed so as to develop the role to a suitable standard.

- Examiners will need to be trained to assure consistency: such training might include the principles of OSCEs, an opportunity to watch and practice mark videos of previous OSCEs, practice marking of live stations (and trying out for themselves how stressful OSCEs can be) and discussion of the process of standard setting.

- Boursicot and Roberts advise of some of the things that can go wrong, including the problems associated with using live and sometimes inconsistent patients and a range of operational difficulties, but nevertheless conclude that OSCEs are a really valuable way of assessing practical skills.

(summarised from Boursicot and Roberts 2005)

COMPARISON OF METHODS FOR ASSESSING PRACTICAL LABORATORY SKILLS

Table 7.2 compares methods for assessing practical laboratory skills. How can we choose which methods to use? When designing an appropriate assessment strategy it is helpful to ask:

- Which practical skills are to be assessed in each laboratory?
- Can any of these be assessed synoptically?
- How is each practical skill best assessed?
- Who among those who are available is best placed to assess the practical skill?

These questions may seem obvious at first sight, but many programme designs give little consideration to these questions. For example, where students are required to routinely report standard laboratory practices, the resulting over-assessment can lead to lack of student focus and high assessment loads for a single assessor. Identification of learning outcomes for each laboratory (different foci of assessment for different experiments), consideration of self- and peer assessment, the adoption of computer assisted assessment and other technological innovations, together with a wider appreciation of the diversity of methods available for the assessment of laboratory skills can all have a positive impact on designing effective laboratory-based assessment.

75

■ TABLE 7.2 Comparison of methods for assessing practical laboratory skills

Method of assessment	Features
Traditional lab write-up report where students submit lab reports post hoc, weekly or fortnightly.	Gives students frequent practice in writing lab reports. Instils a disciplined approach to measuring and recording results. Provides a detailed record. Can give students regular feedback (but may remain largely unread). Risk of plagiarism of lab results from peers and previous years' students. Bright students often organise themselves into consortia and share out the work. Provides a high marking burden for staff.
Laboratory diary/logbook.	Completed during the laboratory session, not outside the laboratory at a later time, ensuring there is no loss of data and that the laboratory diary is the work of the student. Can be a time-consuming and burdensome task for staff and students. It can often be seen to be an over-assessment of the students' work. Modern versions require students to complete lab diaries on PCs or laptops within the lab and to submit them electronically, in the best cases with automated checking and feedback.
Objective structured clinical examination (OSCE).	Students rotate through a series of stations where they are asked to perform procedures. Requires detailed planning.
Observation of students performing a practical task within the lab.	Can be thorough, but is time- and staff-intensive. Students may behave differently when the tutor is not watching them.
Demonstration of a practical skill.	A fast and reliable way of assessment and feedback, but time consuming.
Oral viva/presentation of results.	Guards against plagiarism. Can be probing. Useful to ascertain whether the student has understood the practical work they have carried out. Immediate feedback is given at the time of the oral assessment. However, this is time-intensive and can be logistically challenging to organise.
Simulation exercises (including live simulations with actors or real patients/samples and computer-based simulations).	Supports practice and can be reasonably authentic but not totally so. Can be time- and resource-intensive to set up.

Some suggestions for assessing practical skills in laboratories:

- **Consider strategies for reducing student workload in producing lab write-ups.** Consider providing formats such as tables for students to complete rather than requesting full reports in every lab.
- **Consider strategies for reducing staff workload in producing lab write-ups.** Look to ways to reduce the number of reports, for example by sample marking or marking different aspects of reports, or by requesting team rather than individual report submissions.
- **Consider alternatives to traditional lab write-ups** especially where it is important to assess practical laboratory skills rather than knowledge of the skills.
- **Consider how students will use feedback.** Review how students use written feedback, and if it is not used find other, more effective ways to deliver formative feedback. There is little to be gained from investing time and energy in providing comment that is never read. Consider the merits of involving students in peer assessment.

ASSESSING SKILLS IN COMPUTER LABORATORIES

A range of practical skills can now be assessed in a computer lab. Popular culture has adopted many of these applications, ranging from equipment measuring golf swing and kit, to measuring the technical mastery of a musical instrument. Virtual reality now offers students in some HEIs the opportunity to perfect practical skills in a safe environment, for example keyhole surgery for novice surgeons using simulated patients.

Computer labs offer huge potential for rich, interactive and inter-esting assessment. The use of computer-aided assessment as a formative resource is being recognised across the breadth of HE and a body of research is building up surrounding its use. A common use of the computer lab is as a host for computer-assessed multiple choice, or similar tests. Used formatively, with text boxes giving students reasons why their answers are right or wrong, tests of this type offer flexible, on-demand, directed support to students throughout a programme, as well as easing the assessment burden for staff testing students' under-pinning knowledge. The initial design of tests and the production of the test bank of questions will be time-consuming and must be planned with care. However, there are now numerous test banks of questions available in every area with the potential for the sharing of questions available through most HE academy subject centres in the UK and via professional and subject bodies (PSBs) in many other countries.

 Case study 7.3

The University of Luton has been using CAA formatively for many years to very good effect. Among the specialised exam set-up adaptations they have included are:

- fitting baffles on the sides of machines to ensure students can't look across to the screens of other students;
- presenting questions to students in a different order, so they can't work in tandem if working in sight of one another;
- sitting students taking different tests alongside one another, again to avoid cheating;
- requiring students to leave coat, mobile phones and headwear (other than that worn for religious reasons) outside the computer lab;
- requiring invigilators to be especially vigilant.

Computer-assisted examinations can be valuable in assessing live and practical skills in some circumstances, particularly where simulations are used. CAA offers benefits in terms of reduction of repetitive marking, no inter and intra tutor reliability problems and the elimination of personal bias. It can provide very fast (and formative) feedback to students and is particularly good for students who don't write fluently. Question types which go beyond multiple choice questions, and are therefore suitable for assessing live and practical skills, include drag and drop questions, choosing correct items from a menu, labelling diagrams, using case studies, using simulated patients and demonstrating simulated skills like keyhole surgery and flight simulation.

CAA can never be a quick fix, however, and requires substantial investment to produce good assessments. Design teams for CAA should include excellent content originators, pedagogic experts and designers who have good technological capabilities. This is rarely a task which is done well by individuals. The benefits of CAA need to be counterbalanced by disadvantages, including potential security problems with student hackers, and practical problems with room availability and IT failures. However, the main benefits of CAA lie in the potential for extensive formative feedback, with responses to student work potentially automatically generated by email. Students seem to really like having the chance to find out how they are doing, and attempt tests several times in an environment where no one else is watching how they do. A further advantage is that tutors can monitor what is going on across a cohort, enabling concentration of energies either on students who are repeatedly doing badly or those who are not engaging at all in the activity. Harvey and Mogey in Brown *et al.* (1999) have really helpful advice on the pragmatics of CAA.

 Case study 7.4

The programming team in the School of Computing at Leeds Metropolitan University have for some years made use of computer aided assessment to support learning of lower level skills. Having found that many students benefit from repetition of basic programming exercises in the early stages of a software engineering course, automated formative assessment of these skills was introduced. Systems have been developed that automatically test and verify the student code and then provide immediate feedback to the student about the performance of their code. A marked increase in student learning of these practical skills has resulted. The team also routinely use software plagiarism tools to analyse code and highlight matches and degrees of matches between work submitted by students for summative assessment. At higher levels, programming tasks are less tightly specified, allowing students to be more creative (for example in producing an adventure game or interactive website). Here students are encouraged to help each other and formatively to peer assess each other's programs. A time-constrained practical programming test ensures that collaboration is regarded by students as a developmental opportunity.

(Simon Sharpe, Innovation North Faculty, Leeds Metropolitan University)

Today there are sophisticated ways of involving computers in the assessment of live and practical skills. One interesting area is the support of group work, peer and self assessment of group work and facilitation of cross-level, cross-site and synoptic assessments. The work of CETL ALiC (the Centre for Excellence in Teaching and Learning for Active Learning in Computing (www.dur.ac.uk/alic), one of 74 CETLs in the UK) is looking to further develop work in this area.

Discussion boards, web forums and other web applications that provide space for written 'discussion' between groups of students can be helpful in providing an auditable and assessable discussion trail in teamwork. Individual student input to ideas generation, planning, and other team discussions can be read and contributions assessed. This is particularly useful where teams are perhaps geographically dispersed and are communicating exclusively via the discussion board.

Some tips on using computer-aided assessment (CAA) formatively:

The following tips give some initial guidance on using CAA: more information can be gained from Brown *et al.* (1999).

- **Work out how you will ensure parity in computer-based tests.** Care has to be taken in designing computer-based tests as there are additional considerations over and above traditional exams. For example, resource constraints can sometimes dictate that students must sit the test in different venues at different times. There is always the danger of computer failure during a test and, where it has not been possible to isolate the lab, of some students surreptitiously accessing resources perhaps via the internet during a test.

- **Consider invigilation issues for computer-based tests.** The physical layout of many computer labs means that students can often hide behind their machines and toggle between applications, unbeknown to tutors. It is not always possible to reorganise the layout of a computer lab for a test and it is therefore important to ensure there are sufficient numbers of invigilators.

- **Develop a large test bank of questions and consider selecting a different sub-set for each student.** If it is not possible to schedule students to sit a computer-based test at the same time in the same room, ensure you have a large test bank of questions from which to devise similar but different tests for different sets of students.

- **Ensure students sitting computer-based tests are correctly identified.** It is particularly important to verify the identity of students sitting computer-based tests as there is no handwritten submission and their identification may not be checked after the event. Photo ID can helpful, but should be checked against student numbers to guard against impersonation.

Chapter 8

Assessing the production of artefacts in the studio and workshop

The production and assessment of artefacts is core to many vocational courses. In some domains it is necessary to assess technical accuracy, in others creativity or originality, and in others it is the assessment of the production process rather than the artefact itself which is important.

TECHNICAL ACCURACY

On an engineering course, students might be expected to produce a piece of turned metal or weld a joint in the workshop. Students on a built environment course might be asked to plumb in a toilet during an initial induction programme. Electrical engineers might be expected to show familiarity with basic wiring and system design. Fashion students would expect to be able to demonstrate accurate fabric and pattern cutting. Prior to widespread usage of computer-aided design (CAD) packages, high levels of competence in technical drawing were requirements for both architecture and engineering undergraduates. In some of these domains creating artefacts with high levels of accuracy is highly prized. In other areas it is more important to show an understanding of the techniques involved in producing the artefact. In other words, sometimes we may wish to technically assess the artefact and at other times assess the techniques used in production of the artefact. It is clearly important that we establish which, if either, of these is our objective before designing our assessment of technical accuracy.

Where it is the case that assessment of technical competence is at the centre of the experience, it is important that students have plenty of opportunities for practice, that feedback is timely and frequent to enable the remediation of errors and that students have frequent recourse to examples of what constitutes good practice.

CREATIVITY

One of the most complex areas of assessment is in the domain of aesthetic judgement. The nature of the assessment process is very different when assessment decisions are being made not so much on a basis of right and wrong, as might be the case in (low level) mathematics, but on issues such as originality, creativity and beauty. Whilst tutors in these domains correct work and remediate errors, just as any other tutor would, their job in assessing artefacts is more likely to additionally involve evaluations based on their experience and expertise, and even taste. One can comment on the cutting or finish of a fashion item if the aim is to provide a faultless garment, but if the desired effect requires fraying hems and ragged cutting, a different value base is required. An unsophisticated piece of sculpture might be regarded as technically without fault, but lacking in aesthetic appeal, while anatomical accuracy and smoothness of welded finish are not considered prerequisites of outstanding work by acknowledged geniuses like Henry Moore or Anthony Gormley.

Where creativity is a major feature of an assessment it is important that subjectivity is made explicit in the judgement. Assessment by panel rather than individual can go some way to countering the effects of personal taste.

 Case study 8.1

Within one core module at the Institute for Enterprise, Leeds Metropolitan University, the students are encouraged to use creative and technical skills to create a commercially viable new product from their discipline areas – be that a software solution, a piece of music or a new technological device. A parallel module teaches entrepreneurial skills and asks the students to assess the feasibility of the product, working through an entire business planning phase to determine whether their product has a market. Marks are awarded for these modules jointly and assessment is made not only by the academic staff but also by a panel of invited external assessors who attend the final showcase. High marks can be achieved by creative thinking and solid business analysis, and therefore if the outcome or product of the first module does not have a customer base or market this will not preclude the student from achieving good marks. The symbiotic nature of this assessment is designed to encourage students to draw from both modules to ensure that their product is created with the cost constraints of manufacture or delivery in mind.

(Alison Price, Head of Enterprise Education, Institute for Enterprise, Leeds Metropolitan University)

ORIGINALITY

Judging whether an artefact demonstrates originality is another potential minefield. Found objects often comprise significant elements in artworks, and evaluating their use is complex. Duchamp was able to use a urinal wittily as an original artwork and Picasso combined elements of a bicycle to represent a bull, but only these first usages are incontrovertibly original artefacts. The second user of bathroom porcelain might claim to be acting in homage to the master, but to what extent could that be regarded as creative?

Difficulties can arise when a student believes what s/he is doing is original, without realising that it has been done before in a domain familiar to the assessor but unknown to the student. In a post-modern age, where quoting others' work is grist to the mill, it is sometimes very difficult to draw the line between homage and plagiarism, quoting and copying, especially since intentionality is very difficult to evaluate. With sampling as part of the dominant music culture and advertising making extensive use of a wide range of cultural references, it is often difficult to unpick the origins of artistic inspiration.

Clear guidance regarding acceptable practice and appropriate supervision of students throughout the development process may go some way to ensuring that unintentional plagiarism is avoided.

Collective production is not uncommon in the artistic domain, and yet HE systems often find it difficult to cope with assessment of artefacts produced by more than one person. It can be difficult to extricate the individual achievement in, for example, a collaborative installation, a film or a jointly designed and produced mural. Yet if our assessment systems are to be authentic, they need to be able to accommodate artistic means of production as experienced in the real world.

 Case study 8.2

Students on the BA (Hons) Television Production programme at Bournemouth Media School work in groups to produce TV projects replicating industry practice. The group dynamics work on two levels – shared responsibility for the assignment, and an industry hierarchic model of a director, producer, camera operator, and so on, all having different levels of technical and/or creative responsibility. Students are assessed by three means: a shared mark for the final product, individual production analysis of the process and final product, and peer assessment using an online peer assessment tool that has a focus on developmental, formative learning, feedback and summative assessment.

(Andrew Ireland, National Teaching Fellow, Bournemouth Media School)

Vivas and group walk-throughs of work are often helpful in illuminating the extent and nature of individuals' contributions, particularly where the tutor allows the students to freely discuss the collective process among themselves.

Inclusive approaches to assessment can provide particular issues when applied to the production of artefacts. Disabled students may face particular challenges in the production of artefacts, requiring manual dexterity for example, and reasonable adjustments will need to be made which nevertheless maintain the required standards and achieve the learning outcomes of the programme.

As with other forms of assessment, it is imperative that all students receive clear guidance on the required learning outcomes for a programme of study which requires the production of artefacts. The assignment brief will need to be clearly, fully and constructively aligned to these specified outcomes without over-prescribing what is required (sometimes called in other contexts a 'painting by numbers' approach, which would be particularly inappropriate here!). High levels of independent activity are frequently the norm when students are working in the aesthetic domain, and regular and constructive formative feedback is often the principal means of guiding learning.

 Case study 8.3

In one approach to assessing artefacts, used by one of the authors, students work in teams of five with a brief to design and produce an artefact from the same (limited) resources. The teams are in competition for an imaginary tender. Assessment is via a showcase, where each team is given a stand to display their artefact. Each team is visited by a large number of diverse assessors (tutors, faculty management, invited guests from other faculties, local entrepreneurs and other external guests) throughout the showcase. Each assessor spends a maximum of three minutes at each stand. The students therefore develop a verbal pitch to explain and justify their artefact and to convince each assessor that they are the most creative, innovative and technically competent team and should be awarded the tender. Students are familiar with the showcase feedback sheet that assessors complete.

The advantages of the approach outlined in Case Study 8.3 are:

1   Students develop key skills in teamwork, project management and presentation skills.
2   The large number of assessors ensures students are not unfairly affected by the subjective taste of one individual examiner.
3   Students report they find the experience enjoyable.
4   It provides authentic assessment. Often creative domains are highly competitive and it is necessary for students to be able to make an immediate impression (for example, in creative technologies such as computer games programming it is common practice for final year students to develop 30-second DVD/CD based portfolios to mailshot to prospective employers).
5   Students have the opportunity to learn from the various approaches and artefacts of other teams.
6   The necessity for students to justify their artefact ensures they reflect upon their choices.
7   Assessment is relatively undemanding, based *explicitly* upon personal impression (of a large number of individual assessors).
8   Assessment is efficient. Each assessor may assess up to 20 teams per hour (although a large number of assessors are required).
9   Feedback to students can include the actual sheets from assessors, which allows each student to reflect upon the range of opinion.

Tips on assessing the production of artefacts:

■   **Clarify the standard of achievement that is required.**
Help students to understand what level of basic capability is required, with authentic examples for comparison wherever possible.

87

Showcase Feedback Sheet

Assessor name: ....

Assessor description: ....

Team name: ....

	Excellent 5	4	3	2	Not evidenced 1	0
Creativity Is the use of materials interesting?						
Originality Is the artefact different?						
Justification Did the verbal pitch/answers to questions explain the rationale?						
Total:						

Total score (maximum 15):

Comments for students:

FIGURE 8.1 Showcase feedback sheet

- **When showing students how to do something as part of your formative guidance, avoid doing it for them, however tempting that might be.** It can be very frustrating for someone who is an expert to watch a novice struggling, but when competence is required students may need to be supported through making a lot of mistakes before they can become experts. It is easy for them to become disheartened if the demonstrator is making what they are struggling with look easy.

- **Where the production of artefacts forms part of the programme of learning, be clear about the extent to which capability is imperative.** For students gaining experience of industrial processes, for example, high levels of competence may be less important than merely having had the experience itself.

- **Provide informative assignment briefs that avoid stifling individuality.** Enable students clearly to understand programme expectations in terms of originality and what that means in this particular context. Use practical examples wherever possible to unpack ambiguities.

- **Ensure that critiques and other forms of formative feedback concentrate on the work rather than the person.** This is good practice in all forms of assessment, but particularly so in domains where students are likely to take feedback very personally, as judgements of their personal worth.

- **Build in cross-cultural capability.** Enable aesthetic judgements to encompass other cultural norms than the dominant one in the assessing institution. This may require considerable 'leg work' by the assessor, but is important if we are to be inclusive.

- **Where applicable, ask the student to demonstrate their artefact.** This allows students to highlight aspects of their artefact and to explain the development process.

- **Where possible, involve the client or end user in an assessment of the product.** This is particularly important where the artefact is intended to be commercial and in these cases perhaps auctions or other sales could be considered as authentic assessment vehicles.

89

- **In creative domains consider the use of assessment panels.** Public displays or showcases may be worth considering in order to gain a shared approach to student achievement that is not dependent on an individual view.
- **In assessing creativity and originality it is often helpful to have students submit drawings and other supplementary evidence of the design and development of the artefact.** This can be helpful in providing a rationale for the artefact and can also show the process by which the artefact/production was achieved.

Chapter 9

Assessing live performance

Live performances make up significant proportions of many arts degrees including music, dance and theatre studies. There can also be proto-performance elements within law, marketing and other related degrees where marks are given for time and location-specific individual and/or collective outputs. Additionally there are often requirements to assess live performance on professional courses. Regardless of context, live performance is essentially ephemeral and as such can be one of the hardest areas to assess fairly. There are always going to be debates regarding the relative importance of objectivity and subjectivity, of accurate interpretation over creativity and of product versus process in the assessment of live performance. Ensuring reliability of assessment is particularly problematic in assessing live performance as by nature no two performances will be the same. Even in the assessment of a single performance, critics frequently disagree.

There is also, of course, the extent to which it is possible to assess individual performances that form part of a complex, integrated production; and whether in an individual performance it is desirable to assess the performance holistically or to analyse different aspects separately from the whole. Issues of originality discussed in Chapter 8 apply here too. It may be difficult to evaluate how original a contribution may be within a predetermined script or musical score, particularly when the director or conductor is firmly controlling the way the performance is played, and may not welcome virtuoso improvisations.

When students are preparing and presenting their own original work, for example in dance or music, it can be problematic to differentiate between homage and plagiarism. Students will need to be carefully guided so they are aware of the boundaries of acceptable behaviour. There is a host of issues and possible perspectives to be considered when designing assessment. Are we assessing the piece or the performance? Can we separate the performance from the script/choreography/text, etc.? Would people pay to see this performance? Would I employ this performer?

Given all the variables and potential problems associated with the assessment of live performance it is important in the first instance to develop clear learning outcomes and assessment criteria as a starting point for assessment. However, in creative areas in particular, there is sometimes a need to recognise and to credit performances which are outside the assessment framework.

Performance anxiety is likely to play a significant part in assessments, and caveats concerning stress and mental health issues as outlined in Chapter 3 will need to be borne in mind. It is worth noting that not all students on performance-related programmes will go on to be perform-ers themselves on graduation: they may take up roles within production, direction, management and design, for example. However, since per-formance will make up significant parts of many of these graduates' ultimate working lives, it is neither sensible nor desirable to over-compensate. We should instead take all possible steps to support students.

Nine steps towards fair assessment of a live performance:

1 Ensure health and safety precautions are taken and a risk assessment is carried out.
2 Give, or negotiate with, students clear assessment criteria and access to the marking scheme.
3 Ensure the environment, the location, lighting and soundproofing are adequate and consistent.
4 Ensure technical support is on hand as necessary.
5 Where subjective judgement is required, consider the use of a panel of assessors.
6 Make students aware of the make-up of the panel in advance wherever possible.
7 On some occasions consider excluding the tutor from the assessment panel in order to reduce the halo effect by which judgement is based on previous knowledge of the student.
8 Where possible allow students to rehearse in the room in which they are likely to be assessed, to enable familiarisation.
9 Provide opportunities for developmental formative feedback leading up to the performance.

Case study 9.1

Geoffrey Baxter of the University of Ulster describes using hypnotherapy and relaxation techniques to reduce performance anxiety and thus enhance musical performance. Students in the study reported feeling less anxious when playing, felt better able to concentrate and had improved levels of confidence and self-belief. They seemed better able to combat negative self-talk and used creative visualisation techniques to help make assessed performances less stressful, and even enjoyable.

> Much of the anxiety musicians suffer in assessment situations appears to be controllable, and so it seems that a change in attitude can bring about a better quality of performance and a better experience for the performer. Many students and musicians find that their performing lives are made unnecessarily more difficult through anxiety and although hypnosis is not a substitute for the hard work and preparation musicians dedicate to their profession, it can help in dealing with the stresses of performance, dealing with irrational fears, reinterpreting self-image, focussing attention and increasing motivation to practice. The aim of the hypnosis treatment is to give the musicians the resources to cope with the pressures of performance and ensure that they are equipped to consistently perform to their highest potential.
>
> (Baxter 2004: 130–43)

Students working in groups in performance can be particularly difficult to assess fairly. When casting students for a performance, inevitably the biggest roles will be given to the most able students, who then have the maximum opportunity to shine by comparison with their peers (who are then faced with the challenge of making a walk-on part memorable). Criteria will need to be designed to take into account the opportunities individuals have to make the most of their roles.

Ensemble performances have their place in many performance programmes, with students sharing or rotating roles, but when assessment is aiming to be authentic, particularly when genuine audiences are involved, one has to cast according to individual strengths. Providing students with equivalent rather than identical opportunities to demonstrate their competences can be very difficult.

Case study 9.2

In a level 2 module of a BA Theatre Dramaturgy course at the University of Leeds, students work in groups of three in preparing a performance and are required to support each other as performers or technical assistants. During the process of peer tutoring, each student gives electronic feedback to the other members of their group, including positive comment and recommendations for improvements. Each group of three students then assesses another group's final presentation and applies the discussed criteria. Although the comments do not contribute to the final mark, the feedback is given to students at the end of the module. The advantages of the approach include highlighting the assessment criteria and the assessment process to students.

(HE Academy PALATINE, Dance, Drama and Music.
http://assessing-groupwork.ulst.ac.uk/case_study14.htm)

Assessment of fellow students' performances may be fraught, although peer review is an essential part of enabling students to develop the qualities of judgement necessary to improve their own performance. As always, reliance on evidence of achievement against clearly specified criteria is imperative, supported by opportunities to see and discuss a range of indicative ways in which this can be achieved.

Simulated activity programmes are sometimes used in professional domains where the ability to perform under pressure is a fundamental requirement, for example in the assessment of legal advocacy or surgery. It is a good idea to record these activities not only for quality assurance but also to allow students to reflect upon their own performance, perhaps via reflective journals.

 ## Case study 9.3

Mark Pulman (2004: 75) describes using inter-peer assessment with students on the BA (Hons) in Popular Music Studies at Barnsley College for band performances, with third and sometimes second year student panels assessing first year students' live evening gigs, following practice and training in giving peer feedback. He finds them committed and professional in their approach, with tutor moderation rarely being necessary, and both the students being assessed and those assessing benefit from the experience.

When designing an assessment strategy for a performance-based subject at degree level, a balance needs to be struck between the practical and theoretical elements of the programme. Written work and performance will need to be complementary, with activity supported by intellectual strength. Reflective commentaries are likely to be helpful, where students are able to analyse, synthesise and evaluate their own and each other's performances and to place them within the context of their studies. Those responsible for the validation and approval process for such programmes would be well-advised to require a mixed diet of assessment methods and approaches to ensure validity and rigour. However, formal written assignments should be tailored to be fit-for-purpose rather than included arbitrarily. Written work should be testing and demanding, but always relevant to the discipline and the context.

 ## Case study 9.4

The first of four community theatre practice modules on the BA Theatre Studies course at the University of Ulster requires students to perform as part of a group. Students are given a group mark for the performance. Students are then individually assessed on their ability to self-evaluate their group's performance and peer assess another group's performance. The final assessment of the module requires the student to produce a reflective essay.

(HE Academy PALATINE, Dance, Drama and Music.
http://assessing-groupwork.ulst.ac.uk/case_study2.htm)

 ## Case study 9.5

David Walters of Liverpool Hope University (Hunter 2004) describes the unsatisfactory nature of assessment of performance when two students achieve the same final grade, despite one having made little individual progress from high entry-level ability and another having progressed in leaps and bounds. This led him to look more closely at process assessment to enable him to track and reward added-value. He used a modification of Lin Norton's Ideal Self Inventory (ISI) to help students appraise their own self-development, in the expectation that greater self-awareness would help them achieve higher personal goals. Students also used regularly reviewed

practice diaries to inform the nature and subject content of weekly performance seminars and workshops. It was interesting to note that the process of
getting students to rate themselves on a seven-point scale against 'ideal' and
'not ideal' performance elements threw up considerable divergence between
staff and student views about which were the most important criteria.

Some tips on assessing live performance skills:

- **Work to ensure equivalence in the assessment
  experience.** Inevitably performances can never be identical
  but the assessment process should aim to treat students fairly
  and comparably.
- **Consider offering multiple assessment opportunities.**
  The kinds of skills that are being assessed are likely to be used
  on multiple occasions during a graduate's career, so think about
  observing and reviewing performance on several occasions to
  assure consistency of achievement.
- **Choose the best method of 'recording' the
  performance for the context.** This may literally mean
  recording on video or audio, but could include assessor notes
  (with or without a proforma), peer notes or self-reflection,
  potentially with tutor sign-off.
- **Encourage students to watch their own performances
  on video or digitally.** This can enable students to make
  realistic and accurate judgements of how they are doing so
  long as they are given supportive guidance. It is all too easy
  for excessively self-critical students to become demoralised
  by watching, as they see it, themselves doing everything
  wrong.
- **Encourage formative reflection.** Students can thereby be
  encouraged to focus on potential means of improvement and to
  identify techniques that need further rehearsal.
- **Systematically keep very good records.** You will need to
  retain evidence of achievement for quality assurance and
  moderation processes, and this can be difficult if lots of students
  are involved. Consider how best to store and retrieve evidence
  (in hard copy or digitally) before you start.
- **Clarify benchmarks and standards for achievement.**
  Work with any fellow assessors to articulate what will comprise

Please indicate, by circling the appropriate mark, how you would rate your own performance ability at this point in time. How close do you think you come to your ideal performance?

My ideal performance:		My 'not ideal' performance:
Is well prepared	· · · · · · ·	Is under-rehearsed
Communicates with the audience	· · · · · · ·	Is preoccupied
Portrays confidence	· · · · · · ·	Is obviously nervous
Has charisma	· · · · · · ·	Is timid
Has emotional involvement	· · · · · · ·	Is detached, uninvolved
Has no technical limitations	· · · · · · ·	Highlights inadequate technique
Is musically perfect	· · · · · · ·	Dwells on mistakes

From the list below, please circle the appropriate mark for three more aspects you feel are important for an ideal performance. You may choose not to do so if you are happy that the ideals given above adequately express your performance.

Shows enjoyment	· · · · · · ·	The performer appears to hate it
Has good posture	· · · · · · ·	Looks aimless
Good eye contact/ relationship with audience	· · · · · · ·	Does little to acknowledge the audience
Has clarity of purpose	· · · · · · ·	Lacks concentration
Projects well	· · · · · · ·	Lacks projection
Looks smartly/appropriately dressed	· · · · · · ·	Appears scruffy
Displays good technique	· · · · · · ·	Pieces are too difficult
Has a balanced programme	· · · · · · ·	Has little variety/limited repertoire
Is captivating	· · · · · · ·	Is boring
Has the right notes in the right order	· · · · · · ·	Makes lots of mistakes
Has passion	· · · · · · ·	Is lazy

FIGURE 9.1 The ideal performance inventory

a threshold achievement and how you will recognise sufficient, good and outstanding achievement in the assessed exercise.

- **Work on your intra-tutor reliability.** If you are involved in assessing lots of students demonstrating practical skills over several days (or weeks) you will need to ensure that your own standards don't slip or climb as you become exhausted/exhilarated by the assessment process.

- **Consider the implications of what a loss of anonymity might mean for your marking.** Practical assignments can rarely be marked anonymously (as most written work is nowadays). Be especially vigilant about potential bias when assessing students you know well.

- **Watch out for the 'halo' effect.** Just because a student normally does well in performance, be cautious about over-marking the activity you are seeing at the time of the assessed task. Similarly, don't discount the exceptional performance of a normally lacklustre student as being a fluke.

- **Consider the relative importance of individual and group achievements in assessed work.** Devise marking criteria that reflect what you want students to achieve, whether this is collaborative and mutually supportive (as in a theatrical performance) or idiosyncratic/individual strength (as in a lawyer's mooting competition).

- **When using audience responses as part of the evaluation process, keep the process simple.** Don't expect audiences to make complex and sophisticated judgements based on multiple criteria. You can't hope to brief and train them as assessors, so use them as one part of a multi-agency approach to assessment, in parallel with tutor and peer judgements.

Chapter 10

Assessing process

WHY ASSESS PROCESS?

With the change of focus away from a curriculum centred on what is taught, with assessment of content being paramount, to a focus instead on what is learned, it is inevitable that assessment of process is brought to the fore, particularly when part of the role of the HE assessor nowadays is to provide evidence of employability in graduating students. Employers are keen to be assured not only that the graduates they employ are knowledgeable in their chosen disciplines, but also that they will bring with them to the workplace a range of skills that will enable them to fit in to working teams within the workplace context. These desirable skills vary from subject to subject, context to context and country to country, but generally include the ability to:

- communicate effectively orally and in writing;
- work as a member of a team, demonstrating both leadership and 'followership';
- demonstrate the ability effectively to find and use information from a variety of sources;
- make use of data and demonstrate numeracy;
- use existing and emergent information technologies;
- show initiative and be creative;
- manage one's own time and personal capabilities;
- be a lifelong learner, committed to keeping oneself up-to-date and developing oneself professionally.

To be really effective, these skills need to be shown to be not separate from but integral to subject knowledge, crucially underpinning its application in authentic contexts.

Inevitably, assessment of these kinds of skills is going to require different approaches from those used to assess learned subject content. A focus on 'how' and 'why' as well as 'what' leads to assessment of process as well as product, for example demonstrating how a solution is reached, what alternatives were considered and rejected, what methodologies were used to achieve a particular outcome and often very specifically how individuals worked with one another to achieve the resultant outcomes.

SHOULD WE BE ASSESSING PROCESS AT ALL?

In areas such as clinical practice and social work, assessment of process has long been regarded as a critical and long-established aspect of assessment. In medicine and other health-related subjects, for example, objective structured clinical examinations (OSCEs), which test students' abilities to perform a series of practical activities under time-constrained conditions, are well-embedded in programmes, enabling staff to have confidence in subject-related skills. Similarly in surveying, students are required to undertake lifelike activities using surveying equipment in the field to demonstrate capabilities that will be transferable to live contexts. In other areas it has been accepted that the quality of the outcome or product, for example an accurate translation of another language or the production of a well-considered business plan, is evidence enough that appropriate and relevant processes have been employed. Certainly there is an argument in many real world contexts that performance can and should be judged via the end product.

Although it is sometimes critical to assess process, in some contexts product alone may lend itself to assessment. Indeed there is an argument that it is dangerous to move towards over-defining graduateness in terms of an ability to employ good processes rather than of possession of knowledge and ability to produce outcomes relevant to that discipline. An ability to 'go through the motions' is of questionable value in a computer programmer, for example, since the demonstration of underpinning knowledge and understanding of systems is crucial.

We need to consider carefully when it is our role as tutors to assess process and of what benefit it is to the student or to society to focus attention on assessing process rather than the outcome achieved. At each assessment opportunity it is important to be clear about what we are assessing – outcome or process – and to have a clear rationale for the decision, rather than automatically assuming that process assessment is essential in all cases.

USING ASSESSMENT TO HELP US KNOW OUR STUDENTS

Today, it is not unknown for emails to circulate entire university departments asking 'Does anyone recall this student?' In many HE establishments it is no longer possible, if it ever was, for tutors to spend sufficient time with individual students to be able to form judgements about their attitude or approach. Larger cohort sizes, off-campus demands (particularly the necessity for many students to work in paid employment alongside their studies) and the move towards e-learning have decreased face-to-face contact time. In short, Widening Participation has in many cases led to tutors knowing their students less well.

This is coincidental with a movement towards strategic learning resulting from the increased demands on student time from earning, caring or other responsibilities. A result of this is that students can, in the worst instances, be known largely as an undifferentiated mass from whom anonymous assignments are received and marked, without significant interpersonal interaction. Yet we know that such interaction can be crucial for student motivation and retention.

If our knowledge of our students is being reduced to assessment of outcomes, and if external pressures are resulting in more students adopting a strategic approach to their studies, then these students are likely to focus their energies on simply achieving the outcome being assessed. It must therefore be tempting for them to take advantage of the opportunities available to bypass a non-assessed process stage.

PLAGIARISM

Much has been written elsewhere (for example Carroll 2005) about the increase in students who plagiarise HE assignments, either through ignorance of what is and what is not acceptable or for more nefarious reasons. A number of strategies have been proposed (McDowell and Brown 2001) but the most effective one is to design it out by making assignments difficult to plagiarise. One way of doing this is to focus less on product and more on process. If students are required to demonstrate (and be assessed on) work in progress or collective achievement, it is less likely they will buy assignments from essay factories or download semi-relevant material from the web and pretend it is the product of their own endeavours.

Plagiarism is reportedly on the increase in higher education (Carroll 2005). As it has become easier for students to obtain materials and to

101

deal in final products through digital media, the Internet, photocopying and scanning, it is more appealing for some students to bypass the process stage altogether.

One reason therefore for the increasing interest across HE in assessing process is to ascertain how an outcome has been derived and to ensure that the work that is being assessed is the student's work. The increase in group work on many HE courses has led to similar challenges for tutors in ascertaining the origin of the final group product or outcome. It is not always clear how or even if a particular student has contributed to the group product.

There is much written about the assessment of group work (Brown *et al.* 1994). In an earlier book in this series on small group teaching Kate Exley and Reg Dennick (2004) discussed four basic assessment approaches that can be used to assess students working in groups – individual assessment, same mark allocation, divided mark allocation and self-assessment of teamworking skills. There are problems associated with each of these approaches, but what is most important is that both tutor and students are entirely clear about which method is to be used and why.

If individual contribution is to be assessed, it is important that the criteria are clear from the outset. It is also important that the tutor recognise that the type of assessment approach adopted will in many ways determine the nature of student application to the group process. Many students equate what is valued with what is assessed and where process is judged by academic staff to be important so it should be explicitly assessed.

Assessment of process must be one of the most demanding of assessments for tutors both in terms of time and the resources involved. The main difficulty in assessing process is the logistics of accurately and fairly assessing any activity that, by its definition, may take a significant amount of time to complete.

ASSESSMENT DESIGN

The burden on staff if assessment is ill-designed is excessive so we need to ensure that it is undertaken well from the outset, and this normally means that individuals are not best placed to do it alone, since peer commentary is invaluable in preventing design mistakes.

It may be that it is not possible to design a completely efficient or effective tutor assessment of process, so compromises may need to be made. If we reach the conclusion that it is impossible to measure process accurately then we have to ask the following questions:

- Should process be measured?
- Who is best able to assess process?
- What is the best way of assessing process within the constraints available?

A number of approaches are available to the tutor to alleviate the assessment burden and to ensure assessment is as valid and reliable as possible.

First, it is often more appropriate and/or more practicable to involve others in the assessment. Principally this could include the student themselves and the student's peers but may also include other agencies, including students from other levels in the course or from other courses, plus employers, clients and other stakeholders.

Second, it may not be necessary to observe and assess the entire process lifecycle of an assignment. Sampling, using vivas, and even written examinations in which questions about process are asked all potentially offer alternatives to observation.

In each case we must ask who is best placed to assess the process in a particular context, and to allow assessment if feasible by this best placed agent, with the tutor moderating. This may well be both more efficient and more reliable than tutor observation alone. Whichever approach is adopted, it makes good sense to keep the assessment system as simple as possible, as too many separate components make it difficult to arrive at a final mark.

The remainder of this chapter considers alternative approaches in more detail.

UNSEEN TIME-CONSTRAINED EXAMS

These are still widely used in assessing live and practical skills, largely because they are relatively easy to administer and manage and because markers recognise the format and understand what is required of them; many believe this is the best means by which students can be given, fairly, an equivalent experience and professional and subject bodies certainly value them.

However, they are not normally the best method of providing an authentic assessment of live and practical skills, particularly if they ask students to write about something rather than demonstrate capability. At best, this can only be a proxy for authentic assessment. Additionally, although they are commonly perceived as an antidote to plagiarism, cheating still happens in written exams. Further arguments against them are that they offer a pressured environment, unlike most life experiences where live and practical skills are demonstrated, and that some students, for example those with dyslexia or visual impairments, are heavily disadvantaged by the format.

Nevertheless, some contexts require their use as part of a mixed diet of assessment. If we are to use written exams to assess live and practical skills, we must ensure that the language used in question design and opening rubric is well-crafted. Open rather than closed questions offer authentic response opportunities and those setting exams should consider what they are trying to achieve when deciding the number and type of questions (essays, short answers, mind-maps, diagrams, calculations).

Where unseen time-constrained exams are an obligation, some variants can be used to assess skills and practice effectively:

- **In-tray exercises** are a means of assessing students' abilities to prioritise and work with unknown documentation, emulating the real-life work experiences of, say, an accountant or a ward manager in a hospital encountering a dossier of papers in the morning's mail and having to decide how to deal with them. Typically students are given a bundle of assorted papers at the start of the exam, but no question paper in the first instance, so the exam begins with reading/sorting time. After an interval of perhaps 15 minutes, the lead exam question is introduced, for example 'draw up a trial balance for company x' or 'put together a treatment plan for patient y'. Students are then expected to commence producing responses. Other data can be introduced at intervals throughout the exam as the situation changes; for example, 'company z has now gone out of business: how does this impact on company x?' or 'there has been a major traffic accident nearby: how does this change your ward management plans?' In-tray exercises work well at putting students into lifelike situations that emulate practice to a certain extent, and have proved popular with students and staff. Preparing the dossier of papers can require extensive work, but once put together the materials produced for one cohort can be used in subsequent years with different lead questions.

- **Open-book exams** are useful when assessing students'
  use of information rather than their recollection of it, and
  this can be particularly suited to skills and practice assessment.
  Typically, students are allowed to take whole
  books, part texts or own notes into exams for use as
  reference sources. The focus of questions then is on use of
  information, not recollection. However, students will need
  guidance on the concept of open book exams otherwise
  some, not understanding the concept, may simply try to
  copy out text.
- **Take-away papers** can be used when the focus is on
  demonstrating the application of knowledge rather than its
  recall. Students collect the exam paper at a given time,
  then return it with their answers at a set time. During the
  assessment period, they can visit libraries, websites and use
  a range of information, including consultations with managers,
  mentors and peers. Take-away papers offer high validity, but
  the questions need to be framed carefully to ensure students
  focus on the demonstration of achievement of skills. One
  disadvantage of take-away papers is that it can be harder to
  guarantee that answers are the students' own work as they
  are undertaken off site, but again linking the question to
  students' own practice is helpful. Take-away papers
  disadvantage students with high home caring responsibilities,
  so care needs to be taken in timing take-away papers
  sensitively (for example, avoiding half-term weeks for
  mature students with child-care responsibilities).
- **Vivas** (*viva voce* or oral exams) are more widely used in
  some countries than others and can be very helpful for
  assessing skills and practice in an exam context since
  they offer opportunities to test students on a one-to-one
  basis, test the individual in a live situation and offer chances
  to probe understanding. Typically, questions are asked of an
  individual student to probe understanding of the theoretical
  basis of practical work and to enquire about the process
  of artefact or performance development. However, they
  can disadvantage some students and pose problems for
  students from cultural backgrounds where one-to-one
  interaction, particularly between genders, can be
  problematic.

OBSERVATION

Evaluating process skills by watching them being performed and judging successful achievement of outcomes is a recognised part of assessment in many disciplines, with the advantage of authenticity, but the disadvantage of being very demanding of assessor time. Additionally, we must be aware of the potential halo effect where our knowledge of the person being observed can colour, positively or negatively, our judgement of the performance. In addition, it is an established phenomenon that the very act of observation is likely to affect the process being observed, since people tend to perform differently when being watched.

Where a process is considered critical to professional competence or fitness to practice, for example the ability to deal with a patient sensitively when carrying out a clinical procedure, there is little alternative to observation (although in this case the patient may well be able to be involved in the assessment and feedback). In some cases, however, it may be impossible for tutors, particularly with large student cohorts, to carry out time-consuming observation of students throughout the whole process of them producing deliverables, so proxy assessments will need to be devised.

Peer observation can be much less threatening, but will need careful preparation of both the observers and the observees to ensure that feedback and evaluation are carried out sensitively and appropriately.

SAMPLING

If we choose carefully what we really wish to assess, we may be able to design short assessment tasks that primarily measure this. For example, when assessing lab write-ups students could submit weekly reports throughout the year in the knowledge that only a sample (chosen at random) would be summatively assessed, with each of these samples being reviewed for a different aspect. The opportunity would then exist for tutors to review formatively work submitted by students about whom they had concerns in a non-threatening way. This method can be efficient of staff time as we are not evaluating the same thing again and again, and can result in students taking care with each piece of work submitted. However, students have been known to gamble in these situations, and it is not unknown for copying and plagiarism to be widespread when students know there is an outside chance they will be caught.

SELF-REFLECTION

The strongest argument for the use of self-reflection as a basis for assessment of process is that students alone can assess how much effort they have put into a task and identify all the problems encountered during the course of a project. Encouraging students to reflect on experiences and to learn from them is unquestionably a useful formative exercise.

In fact, some argue that a self-evaluation component should be included in each project. With the emergence of electronic diaries or bloggs, video recording, video booths and virtual learning environments, it is now easier than ever for students to record their experience and to submit for assessment. Reflection comprises more than recording experiences, however, and students are likely to need guidance on what they should do to turn raw data about practice into a meaningful reflective commentary.

At the same time, whilst we may wish to include assessment of a project log or work diary, reflective writing may not be ideal for telling the tutor what really went on, since reflection is based on students' selective and sometimes partial accounts. For this reason, many consider it is probably best to use self-reflection in conjunction with other assessment vehicles. Helpful, too, in this context may be a series of prompts to encourage students to look at critical incidents within a period of independent learning.

Box 10.1
SAMPLE QUESTIONS FOR A CRITICAL INCIDENT ACCOUNT

What was the context in which you were working?

What did you actually do?

How did your learning from your programme of study and your wider reading of the literature in the field influence your choices of action?

What happened as a result?

What were the tangible outcomes?

What would you do differently as a result of your experiences?

What have you learned from the experience?

How would you advise others working in similar contexts?

PEER ASSESSMENT

The act of assessing a peer's processes can be good for peer assessors in terms of improving similar skills of their own and learning from the experience of others. Extensive preparation of students for peer review, together with tutor moderation of peer assessment, is, however, important so that students see the process as fair. It is a good idea to make the marking scheme explicit and detailed, providing peers with proformas for marking which clearly align performance to published criteria (Figure 10.1). This helps students to focus on the most important aspects of performance as well as allowing efficient moderation and processing of the marks by the tutor.

INTRA-GROUP PEER ASSESSMENT

The use of peer evaluation systems is well established on many HE courses. When students are working in teams, it is sensible to ask students to assess the contributions made by the team's members to the process, as they have unique access to the experience. Students may need convincing of the value of peer review of their performance as a member of a group, which should concentrate on the benefits of developing personal and group awareness of achievement.

Many of the risks involved in peer assessment may be overcome by providing clear assessment criteria so that students are not able to over- or under-mark their friends and enemies or to allow unconscious bias to slip in. All marks should be justifiable by reference to the criteria, which may need to be debated and unpacked so that expectations of performance are shared.

It is also possible to involve students in assessing each other's self-reflection reports of group work. This should serve to focus individuals on what happened, their actual role rather than what they would have ideally done. It is also quicker for the tutor to moderate student peer assessment than to mark all reports from scratch. Group reflection, as well as encouraging collaboration, may also be helpful in allowing the tutor to assess process.

SHOWCASING

This comprises offering students an opportunity to share with one another what they have achieved, frequently work in progress, so that

Name of Presenter(s)	1	....
	2	....
	3	....
	4	....
	5	....

Name of assessor: ....

Criteria	1 (excellent)	2 (good)	3 (average)	4 (weak)	5 (inadequate)
1 Ability to put ideas across fluently					
2 Ability to use relevant audio/ visual aids effectively and appropriately					
3 Evidence of good preparation of content material, accuracy					
4 Use of an effective range of information sources, including books, journal articles, web pages, experts					
5 Persuasiveness of arguments, ability to convince					

Further comments:

Total score (maximum 25):

FIGURE 10.1 Sample assessment proforma for presentations

they can obtain peer and tutor feedback. Frequently used formatively, it can also be used summatively. The assessment of process, if designed carefully, can be highly formative and helpful to students in further developing their abilities. In the interests of enriching the student experience, a demonstration and examination of a variety of alternative approaches can be desirable. For example, if we involve students in the assessment of each other's posters in a showcasing event, students can see how others have tackled a project and learn from the experiences of the whole cohort rather than just their own work.

In addition to being a rapid way of alerting students to a wide range of approaches, a showcase is an opportunity for students to discuss this process with a variety of assessors and moderators including senior staff, clients, employers and students from different courses. This can result in efficient moderation and assessment. Once again, it is important to use the experience to help students to gain a broader understanding of what is expected of them in terms of achievement, helping them to share expectations of standards with tutors during the period of production.

TRIANGULATION

Perhaps the most reliable of approaches to assessing process would rely not on any one assessor or any one assessment, but upon a combination of self-, peer and tutor assessments. When assessing something as complex as process, triangulation is particularly desirable, and additionally involving students in their own and others' assessment is potentially developmental for all concerned.

Peer assessing is a useful formative activity in developing the skills to self-assess, and conversely peers can be asked to review and comment on self-reflections of other team members.

Intra-group peer assessment of self-reflection could then be monitored by the tutor, perhaps using short vivas or via written examination questions closely related to the practical process.

Some tips on assessing process:

■ **Be clear about why you are assessing process.**
  Consider at the outset, is the process in itself critical? Or are you primarily checking that the product is wholly the result of the student's own work or, in the case of group work, the extent of the student's contribution? The answer to this

question will largely dictate how process should be assessed. In the former case tutor observation might be required, whereas in the latter it may be more useful to involve the student and their peers more in the assessment. It may not always be necessary or desirable to assess process.

- **Be clear about exactly which aspects of process you wish to assess and why.** It is not always necessary to assess *all* aspects of process in every assignment, particularly where identical or similar processes are carried out routinely by students. You may perhaps wish to use a matrix of assessments.
- **Design and communicate clear assessment criteria.** Make very clear where students are expected to collaborate and where not, so they are clear about boundaries between co-working and plagiarism/cheating.
- **Choose your assessment approach carefully.** Accept that many students are strategic and largely assessment-driven in their approach to their work. Student experience is defined more by their assessments than any other factor and this is of particular significance in the assessment of process.
- **Ensure process assessment is efficient for staff.** Make sure that you are ensuring effective use of staff time and resources, reducing the burden on staff wherever possible.
- **Consider who is best placed to assess process.** In some cases this may be the students themselves, or other students in the same group or other groups, or the tutor or other stakeholders, depending on the context and whether the assignment is to be formatively or summatively assessed.
- **Use proformas to ensure process assessment is based on shared values.** This will support efficiency and more effective tutor moderation.
- **Involve the student in reflecting upon their own processing.** If using a written format, give word limits to encourage students to think in a focused way about what they are doing and to reduce the tutor time it takes to read and assess. It is perhaps best to stay away from full reports on process: instead you can ask for summaries in note form or bullet points which can still evidence analysis.
- **Exploit intra peer group assessment.** This is the best means available to access what really went on within the group.

- **Exploit inter peer group assessment.** Fellow students can learn a lot about process requirements by applying assessment criteria to each other's work.

- **Consider the validity and reliability of the process assessment.** This may best be achieved by triangulation of views including tutor, peers, self and others; which may ultimately be tutor moderated.

- **Consider what evidence will be required to demonstrate process outcomes.** This might include written text and video, audio or digital recordings, which will be useful for subsequent reflection and for showing to external examiners or other scrutineers for moderation.

- **Keep the system of assessment as simple as possible (but no simpler!).** Avoid over-simplification as much as excessive complexity. Limit the number of individual elements and keep commentaries concise to ensure efficient use of tutor time and help moderation.

- **Consider varying where assessment of process will take place.** This might include showcasing sessions, classroom critiques, poster reviews and remote evaluation using on-line evidence and proformas.

- **Identify when assessment of process will take place.** Sampling throughout will avoid the 'sudden death' syndrome when all hangs on a single assessment event. Assessment at the end of a project may include a viva which enables the bringing together of a number of disparate elements and is valuable in helping the tutor evaluate individual contributions and depth of understanding.

Chapter 11

Using other stakeholders to assess student achievement

ASSESSING IN AND FOR THE WORKPLACE

Many programmes offered in HEIs nowadays include an element of learning off-campus, in terms of distance learning, work placements, internships and other opportunities to offer authentic learning and assessment experiences that potentially involve assessors other than the tutor.

It is not uncommon in these instances for issues concerning reliability and consistency of assessment to arise, especially where workplace assessors may initially have little familiarity with institutional requirements.

Employers may have very clear views of what they expect of a placement student and these may not always be in close accord with the HEI's requirements. Some employers, for example, will have studied at universities decades ago and may have fixed views of what a placement student should know and be able to do. They may be highly critical of perceived deficiencies and unaware of student strengths in areas that didn't appear on the curriculum in previous years, including for example information retrieval/management and advanced IT skills. Additionally, while most employers are creative and positive about offering worthwhile placements, some employers still see students as cheap labour and, despite promises of variety and relevance to the course studied, offer them routine and unimaginative experiences in the spirit of 'letting students know what a hard day's work is really like'! In all cases, as paid or unpaid employees, placement students will be expected to contribute to the success of the host organisation. Realistically the daily needs of the organisation will take precedence over academic requirements (which is of course the essence and value of the placement). Placement tutors will need to plan carefully in advance to ensure that the learning experience is appropriate and that evaluations of the students' off-site learning are as fair and comparable as possible.

In order to provide a useful and meaningful learning experience on placement, students are likely to need to have:

- clearly articulated placement outcomes, so that both the student and the employer are clear about what is expected of them;
- an identified list of skills and abilities, closely linked to the published learning outcomes for the programme concerned, that the student will be aiming to learn, develop or enhance during the placement;
- measures for tracking of performance over time, so that progress can be self-evaluated and monitored by the employer, mentor and placement supervisor;
- clear time-lines establishing what needs to be achieved by when;
- contingency plans and/or 'helpline' facilities for students or their supervisors to use if things don't go to plan.

An example of an arrangement for support and assessment of an under-graduate placement (taken from the work placement module specification, Business School, Leeds Metropolitan University) is shown in Figure 11.1.

One of the difficulties in using multiple assessors, which is highly likely when students go out on placement, is that it is difficult to assure consistency of marking standards. Activities aimed to foster consistency of placement assessments include:

- providing a comprehensive workplace assessor briefing manual that is detailed yet undaunting and easy to use;
- running training sessions for workplace assessors to familiarise them with expectations and practices. This may not be a realistic option where busy placement supervisors believe they are too hard-pressed to do more than make a place available for a student;
- undertaking visits or establishing periodic virtual conversations to placement students at which views on progress can be triangulated between the student, the tutor and the workplace supervisor;

114

Intended learning outcomes

Upon successful completion of this module students should be able to:

- demonstrate that they have made an appropriate contribution in the workplace, including team working, communication and problem solving as appropriate;
- evaluate and reflect upon their personal development during the placement;
- critically evaluate and reflect upon the practical application of their academic studies in the workplace;
- determine appropriate strategies to support their career aspirations and lifelong learning needs.

Sample skills development and assessment opportunities

	Opportunity to use/ develop	Assessed
PERSONAL SKILLS AND COMPETENCIES		
Self-awareness	X	X
Citizenship	X	X
Change/coping with uncertainty	X	X
Team/group skills	X	X
CIT skills	X	
Written and oral communication skills	X	X
Presentation skills	X	
Listening/feedback	X	
Networking	X	
ACADEMIC SKILLS AND COMPETENCIES		
Questioning and critique	X	X
Reasoning	X	
Problem solving and decision making	X	
CAREER SKILLS AND COMPETENCIES		
Career and opportunity awareness	X	X
Transition skills	X	X
Awareness of employer's needs	X	X

University support will take the form of:

- pre-placement guidance as necessary, for example seminars, liaison with previous placement students including classes in CV writing, interview technique etc. designed to facilitate self development;
- support during the placement. This will include:
  1 the dedicated full-time staff in the placement office;
  2 normally two visits during the placement from a mentor;
  3 dedicated VLE support;
  4 student support networks.

Assessment methods

1 A short report (maximum 500 words). Students will be given an individual deadline which will be shortly after the commencement of the placement. This will allow students to outline what they hope to gain from the placement, the challenges they expect to face, the preparation that they have undertaken and first impressions (20 per cent).
2. A mark awarded by the tutor at the time of a visit after consultation with the workplace supervisor (30 per cent).
3. A reflective log (maximum 2,500 words). Students will be given an individual deadline which will be shortly after the completion of the placement (50 per cent).

FIGURE 11.1 Workplace assessment

- pairing up experienced and inexperienced workplace assessors and brokering opportunities for mentoring of the novice and induction into the HEI home assessment systems.

When faced with so many variables – the organisational context, the assigned role, working conditions, timescale, supervision, and workplace assessor, it is challenging to ensure consistency, fairness and reliability of assessment. It is perhaps beneficial to try to reduce the number of variables, for example reducing or even removing assessment by the workplace supervisor. The number of visiting tutors assigned by the faculty could with some reorganisation and goodwill also be reduced to support consistency of tutor evaluation. An emphasis on student reflection and self-assessment allows students to exploit any placement opportunity, regardless of its quality, and provides evidence for tutor assessment and moderation.

 Case study 11.1

Students studying diagnostic radiography at the University of Central England, Birmingham are assessed partly in a clinical setting. The majority of supervision is facilitated by clinical colleagues rather than academic staff across a large number of hospitals. This does not necessarily make for identical learning experience or clinical practices. The strategy that has therefore been adopted is to ensure that only those aspects of clinical practice skills that can only be assessed within the actual practice setting are assessed in the setting and no grade is given – clinical assessments are only passed or failed in order to establish that baseline competence has been achieved and patient safety is secure. Clinical practice is complemented by the use of clinical examinations based around clinical scenarios and diagnostic image viewing, and the department has developed a virtual learning domain to create simulations and representations of clinical/practical activities.

(Paul Bartholomew, National Teaching Fellow, UCE Birmingham)

INTERNATIONAL PLACEMENTS/YEARS OUT

In many HEIs a year's placement or internship in a different country is not unusual and there are tremendous benefits to be gained for both the individual student and the home and host organisations in terms of broadening horizons and developing international perspectives. Problems can arise, however, if there are divergent approaches to performance and achievement levels between the nations. These might include very different cultural expectations, for example in relation to grades given. In some countries a C grade is an acceptable middle mark and in others it is considered a poor mark. A pass mark of 40 per cent is acceptable in some nations and contexts whereas a minimum of 60 or 70 per cent is expected in others. Discussions about what grades in use actually mean and conversations about benchmark standards are essential.

Similarly, the role of the tutor/workplace supervisor in terms of student autonomy is very different across nations: some expect 18-year-olds to be completely independent adults, in others there are expectations of a figure acting 'in loco parentis', taking care of the student's learning and even behaviour and having 'duty of care' responsibilities. Lack of shared understandings on basic issues such as these can lead to problems when it comes to grading performance on international placements. In all cases, clearly expressed written guidelines are needed on expectations, codes of behaviour and envisaged outcomes, supplemented by live or virtual conversations to check understanding.

Similarly, students on international placements, especially if they are working in environments where they are very much left to their own devices, will usually need support in helping them to make sense of and benefit from the international learning experience.

Personal development planning (PDP) processes can be really helpful here. In the UK and elsewhere PDP is becoming a normal expectation for all students, usually aimed at helping them to become reflective and capable learners, developing their employability capabilities and helping them track and record their own progress across a whole programme.

DIVERSITY OF PLACEMENT EXPERIENCE

Some would argue that there is no such thing as a bad placement, since outstanding students can make the most even of a negative experience. Nevertheless there will always be students who encounter serious difficulties on placements due to circumstances beyond their control, and tutors need to be prepared for the worst. Reports from placement officers suggest that where students have been proactive in finding their own placement, rather than taking up a placement through the placement office, there is an increased probability of major problems with the placement. Whilst this is not surprising, it is unfortunate that enterprising students are disadvantaged and often find they are given little or no credit for a partial placement that ends unsatisfactorily.

 Case study 11.2

'Last year I was the visiting tutor for a student who had found their own sandwich placement (via the internet) at a small or medium sized company. I visited twice during the year and both the student and supervisor appeared to be satisfied with and benefiting from the placement. Almost 40 weeks into the placement the student rang me in tears. The organisation had terminated the placement and had, apparently for financial reasons, replaced the student with a fresher from our own department who had approached the organisation looking for part-time work. The placement regulations in our school do not allow any placement under 44 weeks to be considered for assessment and the student gained no credit on his course for the placement.'

(Alison, school of computing, a large urban university)

PREPARING FOR THE UNEXPECTED

The very nature of the unexpected makes it difficult to prepare for! However, realistically we need to plan around the possibility of:

- workplace closure/redundancy;
- dismissal of the individual (for fair or unfair reasons);
- harassment, bullying or other kinds of unacceptable behaviour towards or by the placement student;
- disaster or emergency (flood, hurricane, fire, hostilities bringing a placement to an abrupt halt);
- unexpected diversions of activity by a hard-pressed employer who commandeers all 'hands to the pump' in times of crisis with little thought about whether such activities meet the placement student's needs;
- replacement of a management sympathetic to student placements with one which is hostile to the concept;
- placement student ill health or bereavement.

When things like this go wrong, the tutor will need to negotiate with the student concerned to ensure that gaps in the core required work experience are filled. Obviously when an alternative placement becomes necessary this will be sought when possible, but where this proves impractical, perhaps because it is nearing the end of the period or when placements have been hard to secure in the first place, then alternatives may have to be considered. These might include similar strategies as those deployed for students unable to gain placements in the first place.

WHAT HAPPENS WHEN STUDENTS ARE UNABLE TO GET PLACEMENTS ON A COURSE THAT REQUIRES THEM?

Sometimes in a crowded placement market it will prove impossible to place some students. In these instances tutors might consider:

- offering work shadowing experiences;
- seeking mini placements in the home HEI together with additional tasks;
- developing simulated placement activities.

In these cases, ensuring that the assessment is equivalent to that of students with traditional placements is essential. It will be necessary for the tutor and the student to return regularly to the stated learning outcomes for the placement to ensure that students learning in alternative contexts are able to achieve the same outcomes by divergent means.

ADDITIONAL OPPORTUNITIES FOR ASSESSMENT BY CLIENT OR OTHER STAKEHOLDERS

There are many opportunities, particularly in the final stages of undergraduate or postgraduate courses, for students to provide a service to the community. Indeed many professional courses require students to have passed an element of this type before they can be accredited. In cases where students are dealing with actual clients (examples include legal advice centres, IT consultancy and dental services) it is worth considering whether the client may be usefully involved in assessment. In some contexts, it may be possible to utilise commentaries by recipients at the receiving end of students' services or actions. For example, when assessing the taking of a history by a trainee solicitor or doctor, safe lifting of patients by health professionals and services provided in the hospitality industry, clients'/patients' views could be sought.

Interesting work has been carried out at Sheffield University Medical School where patients have been trained to assess medical students' practice and diagnoses of their condition. Patients have demonstrated that where a framework of training is in place they are capable of expertly assessing aspects of practice that would be very difficult to assess accurately otherwise.

Similarly, audiences of student productions/performances, viewers of art works, users of leisure or sport services and others can be asked for evaluations. Obviously this will need sensitive handling and careful set up, since we need to ensure that such judgements are made on the basis of sound principles, using the same kinds of safeguards as other occasions where multiple assessors other than academic staff are making grading decisions including careful briefing, training, mentoring, sampling and moderating of marks. Nevertheless, client/stakeholder assessment can have huge benefits in terms of authenticity of assessment of practice.

 Case study 11.3

There has been a long tradition within social work education of simulated role-play approaches to the development of listening and interviewing skills, with students being grouped into triads for the purposes of practicing skills and receiving feedback. However, the improvement seen in confidence and skills is often not matched by their performance when they begin to do it 'for real'. Skills lab work at Staffordshire University has focused on raising the quality of trainee social workers' communication skills. Key themes and principles which were felt to be essential to success were that:

- the people playing the roles of service users should be as authentic as possible;
- there is a need for effective practitioner feedback throughout the process;
- students learn best if they are given opportunities to practice;
- students are their own most effective critics;

120

■ feedback is most useful if it is consistent;
■ students need to place their learning within a theoretical framework.

A programme was therefore designed around students working with paid service users. Experienced practitioners were involved in each session in order to give specific feedback to the students. Each student on the award has three formative solo interviews – one telephone interview and two subsequent face-to-face interviews before they have to complete a summatively assessed interview at the end of the semester. All interviews can be video-recorded to allow students to review and reflect and these reflections are recorded in writing. The programme matches the students with the same service user and practice educator for each of the three sessions, so that trust can be established. Students produce a reflective analysis of their skills development.

Many students have reported that the skills lab programme not only gave them confidence to go out into social work practice, but that when they were engaging with service users many of the lessons they had learned in the simulated setting helped them deliver a far more effective service than they had expected at this stage of their social work careers.

(Bernard Moss, National Teaching Fellow, University of Staffordshire)

The most successful partnerships between external stakeholders and students are often where the benefit is shared. For example the Leeds Metropolitan University's Business Start-up's summer school invites local entrepreneurs to set tasks for students and graduates who are interested in starting their own business. In teams, the students generate ideas for a new product line to fit within the entrepreneur's existing portfolio. Assessment by the client is formative, authentic and useful to the client. Similarly, many vocational areas such as design schools frequently invite briefs from local or national companies. Students, sometimes working in teams, compete for an imagined or actual tender in a competition judged by the external client.

Numerous undergraduate programmes contain a final year project which involves students applying research to a real world problem or the production of an artefact. In many cases there may be an opportunity to involve external clients in the evaluation of the product. Although this scenario shares many of the problems associated with external assessment of students' placements, the benefits to a student about to embark on a career in the sector should be weighed against the requirement

121

for accurate academic assessment. In some domains, the final year project is divided into the two distinct elements of research method, assessed rigorously by an academic tutor, and product development, assessed by a range of stakeholders including external clients.

Suggestions for involving stakeholders in the assessment of live and practical skills:

- **Highlight opportunities for stakeholders to be involved in assessment.** Consider using the press and other channels to publicise the vocational nature of some of the students' work.
- **Develop partnerships with stakeholders.** Use conferences, meetings and other forums to explore contacts and possibilities of working with stakeholders.
  Be creative about finding assessors of live and practical skills. Look at clients, service users, audiences and the general public to comment on some elements of the assessed skill.
- **Ensure that clear assessment guidelines are provided for external assessors.** Where necessary, training should be given in how to interpret and apply the guidelines.
- **Negotiate the assessment with the stakeholder.** Appreciate that their interests are probably not aligned exactly with the requirements of an academic course.
- **Consider providing client–assessor training programmes** to allow clients to assess customer care and other aspects of practice that are difficult to assess by agents other than the client.
- **Clarify which learning outcomes are being assessed.** If, for example, a placement is considered not to be meeting the intended learning outcomes, consider ending the placement.
- **Consider carefully how stakeholder assessments will be moderated.** One would not wish to compromise the authenticity of the assessment, but standards and equivalence need to be assured.

Chapter 12

Assessing skills and practice
The values that underpin our approach

This chapter is designed to pull together the principles on which we have based this book. In summarising them we offer a list that could be used to prompt personal reflection, act as a checklist for those in the process of curriculum design or as a basis for discussion in a staff development session. It represents a counsel of perfection to which we might all aspire, but which might not be achievable in its entirety on every occasion:

- Assignments testing skills and practice should be practically orientated and designed to link closely with the learning outcomes of the programme.
- Assignments should be fit-for-purpose, taking into account the context, the level, the topic and the students.
- Students should be briefed clearly on the purposes and expected outcomes of any assignment, without being over-directed.
- Diverse methods and approaches should be used to provide opportunities for diverse students to excel.
- Assessment of practical skills should be inclusive from the outset, with alternatives for disabled students built in at validation.
- Where possible an element of self- and/or peer assessment should be included to help students foster their own evaluative and lifelong learning skills within a student-centred curriculum.
- Assignments should be devised to maximise formative feedback and make it integral to the learning process in the studio, the lab, the performance venue and the workplace.

- Assignments should be stretching for students, allowing each to maximise potential and enabling tutors to differentiate between different standards of achievement fairly and transparently.
- Assignments should be, and be perceived to be, fair and equitable with no trick questions or hidden traps to catch out the unwary, the unsophisticated or the disadvantaged.
- Assignments should be efficient of staff time, and allow tutors to concentrate on the skilled components of evaluation rather than on repetitive and mindless grading.
- Assignments should be well-paced, with incremental feedback opportunities, a chance for students to remediate early failure and no 'sudden death' where all is lost if a single assignment or practical task is disastrous.
- Authenticity should be the hallmark of the assessment of skills and practice, with high marks allocated to genuine achievement rather than to proxies of achievement.
- Practical skills should be assessed by the most appropriate assessor in the most appropriate location but should be designed where possible to allow tutor moderation.
- Assignment design should foster the development of independent learning.
- Assignments should be interesting.

Above all, we value the opportunity that assessment offers to engage students in deep learning and to enrich the student experience. Nowhere is this potential greater than in well-designed skills assessment, and imaginative approaches to assessing skills and practice may significantly impact upon student engagement and achievement.

Bibliography and further reading

Adams, M and Brown, S (eds) (2006) *Disabled Students in Higher Education: working towards inclusive learning*, London, Routledge.

Anderson, L W and Krathwohl, D R (2001) *A Taxonomy for Learning, Teaching and Assessment*, New York, Addison Wesley Longman.

Anderson, L W and Sosniak, A (eds) (1994) *Bloom's Taxonomy: a 40-year retrospective. Ninety-third yearbook of the National Society for the Study of Education*, Chicago, University of Chicago Press.

Angelo, T (1996) Transforming Assessment: high standards for learning, *AAHE Bulletin*, April, 3–4.

Angelo, T A and Cross, K P (1993) *Classroom Assessment Techniques: a handbook for classroom teachers*, San Francisco, Jossey Bass.

Baxter, G (2004) Using hypnotherapy to enhance musical performance, in Hunter, D *How am I Doing? Valuing and rewarding learning in musical performance in higher education*, Belfast, University of Ulster, 130–43.

Beevers, C E, Foster, M G and McGuire, G R (1989) Integrating formative evaluation into a learner centred revision course, *British Journal of Educational Technology*, 115–19.

Beevers, C E, McGuire, G R, Stirling, G and Wild, D G (1995) Mathematical ability assessed by computer, *Journal of Computing Education*, 123–32.

Beevers, C E, Youngson, M A, McGuire, G R, Wild, D G and Fiddes, D J (1999) Issues of partial credit in mathematical assessment by computer, *Journal of the Association of Learning Technologies* (Alt-J), 7: 26–32.

Biggs, J (2003) *Teaching for Quality Learning at University*, Maidenhead, Open University Press/SRHE.

Black, P (1995) Can teachers use assessment to improve learning? *British Journal of Curriculum and Assessment*, 5 (2): 7–11.

Black, P and William, D (1998) Assessment and classroom learning, *Assessment in Education*, 5 (1): 7–74.

Bloom, B S (1956) *Taxonomy of Educational Objectives, Handbook 1: The Cognitive Domain*, New York, David McKay Co Inc.

Boud, D (1988) Unpublished conference presentation.

Boud, D (1990) Assessment and the promotion of academic values, *Studies in Higher Education*, 15 (5): 101–2.

Boud, D (1995) *Enhancing Learning Through Self-Assessment*, London, Routledge.

Boud, D (2000) Sustainable assessment: rethinking assessment for the learning society, *Studies in Continuing Education*, 22 (92): 151–67.

Boursicot, K and Roberts, T (2005) How to set up an OSCE, *The Clinical Teacher*, 2 (1).

Bowl, M (2003) *Non-Traditional Entrants to Higher Education: 'they talk about people like me'*, Stoke on Trent, Trentham Books.

Brown, G (2001) *Assessment: a guide for lecturers*, The Learning and Teaching Support Network Generic Centre, Assessment Series No. 3, York, LTSN Generic Centre.

Brown, G, Bull, J and Pendlebury, M (1997) *Assessing Student Learning in Higher Education*, London, Routledge.

Brown, S and Glasner, A (eds) (1999) *Assessment Matters in Higher Education: choosing and using diverse approaches*, Buckingham, Open University Press.

Brown, S and Knight, P (1994) *Assessing Learners in Higher Education*, London, Kogan Page.

Brown, S and Race, P (2002) *Lecturing: a practical guide*, London, Routledge.

Brown, S, Race, P and Bull, J (1999) *Computer Assisted Learning in Higher Education*, London, Routledge.

Brown, S, Rust, C and Gibbs, G (1994) *Strategies for Diversifying Assessment*, Oxford, OCSLD Publications.

Brown, S and Smith, B (1997) *Getting to Grips with Assessment*, SEDA Special No 3, Birmingham, SEDA Publications.

Carroll, J (2005) *A Handbook for Deterring Plagiarism in Higher Education*, Oxford, Centre for Staff and Learning Development.

Claxton, J, Mathers, J and Wetherell-Terry, D (2004) Benefits of a 3-way collaborative learning system: action learning, continuous editing and peer assessment, Edinburgh, Paper presented for the BEST conference *Reflection on Teaching: The impact on learning*.

Clegg, K (2002) Assessing failure or failing to assess?, in Peelo, M and Wareham, T *Failing Students in Higher Education*, Buckingham, SRHE/OU Press.

Cowie, B and Bell, B (1999) A model for formative assessment, *Assessment in Education*, 6 (1): 101–16.

Dweck, C S (2000) *Self Theories: their role in motivation, personality and development*, Lillington, NC, Taylor & Francis.

Elander, J, Harrington, K, Norton, L, Robinson, H, Reddy, P and Stevens, D (2003) Core assessment criteria for student writing and their implications for supporting student learning, in Rust, C (ed) *Improving Student Learning 11: theory, research and scholarship*, Oxford, Oxford Centre for Staff and Learning Development.

Erwin, D (1995) *Erwin Identity Scale: manual*, Harrisonburg, VA, Developmental Analytics.

Exley, K and Dennick, R (2004) *Small Group Teaching: tutorials, seminars and beyond*, London, Routledge.

Fallows, S and Steven, C (2000) *Integrating Key Skills in Higher Education*, London, Routledge.

Farrar, V (2006) Equal to the task: disability issues in postgraduate study, in Adams, M and Brown, S, *Disabled Students in Higher Education: working towards inclusive learning*, London, Routledge.

Gibbs, G (1992) *Teaching More Students 4: assessing more students*, Oxford, Oxford Centre for Staff and Learning Development.

Gibbs, G (1999) Using assessment strategically to change the way students learn, in Brown, S and Glasner, A (eds), *Assessment Matters in Higher Education: choosing and using diverse approaches*, Buckingham, SRHE/Open University Press.

Gibbs, G (2000) Are the pedagogies of the discipline really different? in Rust, C. (ed) *Proceedings of the 1999 7th International Symposium Improving Student Learning: improving student learning through the discipline*, Oxford, Oxford Centre for Staff and Learning Development.

Gibbs, G and Simpson, C (2002) *Does your Assessment Support your Students' Learning?* Online. Available HTTP: http://www.brookes.ac.uk/services/ocsd/1_ocsld/lunchtime_gibbs.html (accessed May 2005).

Harding, J (2000) Creating incurable learners: Building learner autonomy through key skills, in Fallows, S and Steven, C, *Integrating Key Skills in Higher Education*, London, Routledge.

Harlen, W and James, M (1997) Assessment and learning: differences and relationships between formative and summative assessment, *Assessment in Education*, 4 (3): 365–79.

127

Higgins, R, Hartley, P and Skelton, A (2001) Getting the message across: the problem of communicating assessment feedback, *Teaching in Higher Education*, 6 (2): 269–74.

Hounsell, D (1997) Contrasting conceptions of essay-writing, in Marton, F, Hounsell, D and Entwistle, N (eds), *The Experience of Learning*, Edinburgh, Scottish Academic Press.

Hughes, I (2004) *Coping Strategies for Staff Involved in Assessment of Laboratory Write-Ups*, Higher Education Academy Subject Centre for Bioscience Volume 3.

Hunter, D (ed) (2004) *How am I Doing? Valuing and rewarding learning in musical performance in higher education*, Belfast, University of Ulster Press.

Hyland, P (2000) Learning from feedback on assessment, in Booth, A and Hyland, P (eds), *The Practice of University History Teaching*, Manchester, Manchester University Press.

James, D (2000) Making the graduate: perspectives on student experience of assessment in higher education, in Filer, A (ed), *Assessment: social practice and social product*, London, Routledge.

Jones, J, Ollin, S, Ireland, A and Johnson-Smith, J (2003) *Group Work Assessment in Media Production: resource pack*, Bournemouth, Bournemouth University.

Juwah, C, Macfarlane-Dick, D, Mathews, B, Nicol, D, Ross, D and Smith, B (2004) *Enhancing Student Learning Through Effective Formative Feedback*, York, Higher Education Academy.

Knight, P and Yorke, M (2003) *Assessment, Learning and Employability*, Maidenhead, SRHE/Open University Press.

McDowell, L and Brown, S (2001) *Assessing Students: cheating and plagiarism*, York, Higher Education Academy.

Marzano, R J (1998) *A Theory-Based Meta-Analysis of Research on Instruction*, Aurora, CO, Mid-continent Regional Educational Laboratory.

Mentkowski, M and associates (2000) *Learning That Lasts: integrating learning development and performance in college and beyond*, San Francisco, Jossey-Bass.

Miller, A H, Bardford, W I and Cox, K (1998) *Student Assessment in Higher Education*, London, Kogan Page.

Moon, J (2004) *A Handbook of Reflective and Experiential Learning*, London, Routledge.

Nicol, D J and MacFarlane-Dick, D (2006) Formative assessment and self-regulated learning: a model and seven principles of good feedback, *Studies in Higher Education*, 31 (2): 199–218.

Norton, L (2004) Using assessment criteria as learning criteria: a case study in psychology, *Assessment and Evaluation in Higher Education*, 29 (6): 687–702.

Oosterveld, P and Ten Cate, O (2004) Generalizability of a study sample assessment: procedure for entrance selection for medical school, *Medical Teacher*, 26 (7): 635–9.

Orsmond, P, Merry S, and Callaghan A (2004) Implementation of a formative assessment model incorporating peer and self-assessment, *Innovations in Education and Teaching International*, 41 (3): 273–90.

Payne, R C and Baggott, G K (2004) Computer-assisted tests to assess procedural and conceptual knowledge. In Ashby, M and Wilson, R (eds), *Proceedings of the 8th International Computer-Assisted Assessment Conference*, Loughborough, Loughborough University.

Peelo, M and Wareham, T (eds) (2002) *Failing Students in Higher Education*, Buckingham, SRHE/Open University Press.

Pellegrino, J, Chudowsky, N, and Glaser, R (eds) (2001) *Knowing What Students Know: the science and design of educational assessment*, Washington DC, National Academy Press.

Pulman, M (2004) Peer assessment in popular music, in Hunter, D (ed) *How am I Doing? Valuing and rewarding learning in musical performance in higher education*, Belfast, University of Ulster Press.

Race, P (1999) *2000 Tips for Lecturers*, London, Routledge.

Race, P (2001a) *A Briefing on Self, Peer and Group Assessment*, Assessment Series No. 9, York, The Learning and Teaching Support Network Generic Centre.

Race, P (2001b) *Assessment: a guide for students*, Assessment Series No. 4, York, The Learning and Teaching Support Network Generic Centre.

Race, P (2001c) *The Lecturer's Toolkit (2nd edition)*, London, Routledge.

Race, P (2005) Assessment driving learning. In *Making Learning Happen*, London, Sage Publications.

Race, P and Brown, S (2004) *500 Tips for Tutors (2nd edition)*, London, Routledge.

Race, P, Brown, S and Smith, B (2004) *500 Tips on Assessment (2nd edition)*, London, Routledge.

Ramsden, P (2003) *Learning to Teach in Higher Education*, London, Routledge.

Robinson, A and Udell, M (2004) *LTSN Engineering Case Study: developing the independent learner*, LTSN/Higher Education Academy.

Rowntree, D (1989) *Assessing Students: how shall we know them? (2nd revised edition)*, London, Routledge.

Rust, C (2001) *A Briefing on Assessment of Large Groups*, Assessment Series No. 12, York, LTSN Generic Centre. Online. Available HTTP: http://www.heacademy.ac.uk/resources.asp?section=generic&process=filter_fields&type=all&id=1&history> (accessed May 2005).

129

Rust, C (2002) The impact of assessment on student learning, *Active Learning in Higher Education*, 3 (2): 145–58.

Rust, C, O'Donovan, B and Price, M (2005) A social constructivist assessment process model: how the research literature shows us this could be best practice, *Assessment and Evaluation in Higher Education*, 30 (3).

Rust, C, Price, M and O'Donovan, B (2003) Improving students' learning by developing their understanding of assessment criteria and processes, *Assessment and Evaluation in Higher Education*, 28 (2).

Sadler, D R (1989) Formative assessment and the design of instructional systems, *Instructional Science*, 18, 119–44.

Sadler, D R (1998) Formative assessment: revisiting the territory, *Assessment in Education: Principles, Policy and Practice*, 5, 77–84.

Sadler, D R (2003) How criteria-based grading misses the point, paper presented at the *Effective Teaching and Learning* conference, Griffith University, Australia.

Sambell, K and Hubbard, A (2004) The role of formative 'low stakes' assessment in supporting non-traditional students' retention and progression in higher education: student perspectives, *Widening Participation and Lifelong Learning*, 6 (2): 25–36.

Sambell, K and McDowell, L (1998) The construction of the hidden curriculum: messages and meanings in the assessment of student learning, *Assessment and Evaluation in Higher Education*, 23 (4): 391–402.

Shwartz, P and Webb, G (2002) *Assessment: case studies, experience and practice from higher education*, London, Routledge.

Tinto, V (1993) *Leaving College: rethinking the causes and cures of student attrition (2nd edition)*, Chicago, IL, University of Chicago Press.

Wotjas, O (1998) Feedback? No, just give us the answers, *Times Higher Education Supplement*, 25 September.

Yorke, M (1999) *Leaving Early: undergraduate non-completion in Higher Education*, London, Routledge.

Yorke, M (2001a) Formative assessment and its relevance to retention, *Higher Education Research and Development*, 20 (2): 115–26.

Yorke, M (2001b) *Assessment: a guide for senior managers*, Assessment Series No.1, York, The Learning and Teaching Support Network Generic Centre.

Yorke, M (2003) Formative assessment in higher education: moves towards theory and the enhancement of pedagogic practice, *Higher Education*, 45 (4): 477–501.

Yorke, M and Longden, B (2004) *Retention and Student Success in Higher Education*, Maidenhead, Open University Press/SRHE.

WEBSITES

http://www.bournemouth.ac.uk/study_support/study_skills.html

http://web.apu.ac.uk/stu_services/essex/learningsupport/On-lineStdSkills.htm

http://www.brunel.ac.uk/~mastmmg/ssguide/sshome.htm

http://www.uea.ac.uk/dos/learning/

http://www.kent.ac.uk/uelt/learning/online/index.html

http://www.lancs.ac.uk/depts/celt/sldc/

http://www.mmu.ac.uk/academic/studserv/learningsupport//studyskills/welcome.html

http://www.open.ac.uk/study-strategies/index.htm

http://portal.surrey.ac.uk/portal/page?_pageid=1078,1&_dad=portal&_schema=PORTAL

http://www.sussex.ac.uk/languages/index.php

http://www.warwick.ac.uk/EAP/study_skills/index.html

http://www2.glos.ac.uk/gdn/disabil/hidden/index.htm

http://www.heacademy.ac.uk/assessment/ASS051D_SENLEF_model.doc

http://www.derby.ac.uk/ciad/dev/links.html

Index